THE ENTITY THEORY OF CONSOLIDATED STATEMENTS

By
MAURICE MOONITZ
University of California
Berkeley

Brooklyn
THE FOUNDATION PRESS, INC.
1951

PREFACE

THIS BOOK was originally published by the American Accounting Association in 1944 as the fourth in its series of monographs. The first printing is now exhausted; the Executive Committee of the Association has courteously assigned its copyright in order to permit this second printing.

Minor changes in typography, grammar, and style have been made, and a few items added to the bibliography. Otherwise the text of the first printing remains unchanged.

MAURICE MOONITZ

September, 1951

PREFACE TO FIRST PRINTING

THE RECENT REVIVAL or interest in consolidated statements has emphasized anew the lack of a firm theoretical foundation on which to build satisfactory multicompany reports. The confusing array of alternative and sometimes contradictory procedures found in accounting literature is one important manifestation of the absence of a generally accepted explanation of the nature, purpose, and limitations of consolidated statements. The present study is an attempt to remedy this deficiency by presenting a theory of consolidation based upon what accountants evidently strive to do, namely, treat a group of closely allied corporations as a distinct economic or accounting entity, despite the existence of legal lines of separation among the constituent parts.

Specifically three important aspects of consolidated financial statements are dealt with: the functions performed by consolidated reports, the circumstances under which they should be presented, and the standards and principles underlying their preparation.

The functions performed by consolidated statements are indicated by examining the conditions which led to their adoption as complements of single company reports. It will be found that consolidated reports, almost uniquely an American device, are limited sharply in their legitimate usage, but that within the area of limitation they serve needs not met by other types of financial statements.

Under what circumstances these statements should be prepared is a question properly answered only after their functions are clearly understood. Because of the generally unsettled status, both at law and in business practice, of intercorporate relations, definite, universally acknowledged indicators of the circumstances calling for their presentation are lacking. In this connection certain criteria sometimes employed are tested in order to develop a set of standards capable of application to diverse corporate interrelationships.

The procedure to be followed in preparing these statements follows logically from their function and purpose. The treatment described in the final section of this monograph is consistent with and derived directly from the earlier conclusions on the purposes for which consolidated reports are prepared.

In addition to the problems involving consolidated balance sheets, income statements, and surplus schedules, considerable attention is paid throughout to the related problems of proper accounting on the books of the individual companies involved, both parent and subsidiary. Little or no emphasis is placed on mechanical phases of the work, as, for example, the forms of work sheet to be employed. Also outside the scope of this study is the problem of the precise technical form (as opposed to content) these reports should take, as well as the related problem of the extent to which reports submitted to agencies such as the New York Stock Exchange and the Securities and Exchange Commission should agree with statements issued to stockholders.

Acknowledgments are due George D. Bailey, Stephen Gilman and William A. Paton, who constituted the Committee on Monographs of the American Accounting Association at the time the present study was initiated, for encouragement and criticism. Professor Paton was especially helpful at all stages of the project. Earle C. King, Assistant Chief Accountant of the Securities and Exchange Commission, was kind enough to offer valuable suggestions before the study actually got under way. Henry R. Hatfield and Perry Mason, both of the University of California at Berkeley, read the preliminary draft of the manuscript and contributed valuable criticisms. Dr. Hatfield was unusually lavish of his time and energy, both through personal conference and detailed written comments.

Needless to say, none of the gentlemen mentioned is responsible for the views herein set forth. On the contrary sharp divergences of opinion emerged on more than one point. The final decision as to the form and content of the study was made by the author; in that sense, and that sense only, this monograph is his work.

MAURICE MOONITZ

September, 1944

CONTENTS

Chapter Page

Preface iii

I. Institutional Background 1

Historical development of holding company in United States. Partial recognition of entity transcending corporate boundaries. Development of use of consolidated statements. Quantitative importance of holding company in United States.

II. Basic Premises 12

III. The Area of Consolidation 20

Percentage of stock ownership as a standard. "Controlling influence" as a standard. Similarity of operations as a standard. National concentration as a standard. Consistency of treatment as a standard. Summary.

IV. Elimination of Intercompany Transactions 40

V. Intercompany Investments and Other Assets 46

Investments in affiliates on owners' books. Elimination of intercompany shareholdings. Intercompany bonds. Reciprocal shareholdings. Assets obtained from affiliates.

VI. Outside Interests; Consolidated Surplus 76

VII. Summary and Conclusions 83

Bibliography 87

Index 93

†

I

INSTITUTIONAL BACKGROUND

CONSOLIDATED STATEMENTS do not exist in a social or economic vacuum. They were developed to fulfill a real need arising out of specific historical conditions; they are the reflections on the accounting level of the distinctive pattern assumed in this country by the combination movement. When those historical conditions alter sufficiently, consolidated statements will be supplanted by forms more congenial to the changed circumstances.[1]

Historical Development of Holding Company in United States

Stimulus to the control of several corporations by means of stock ownership was given by the Sherman Act of 1890, which in effect outlawed the use of the hitherto popular trustee device. The legal means of accomplishing the result prohibited by the Sherman Act were provided in 1893 by New Jersey in amplifying an amendment to its corporation law, originally adopted in 1888, permitting one corporation to hold shares in other corporations.[2]

---

1 ". . . the holding company never assumed the same significance in Europe as it did in the United States. Reasons for this are the more limited use of the stock company as a form of business enterprise and the greater degree of legal regulation and governmental supervision over the formation of corporations, the issue of securities and all other phases of corporate activity. Also the railroads and public utilities, a favorite field for the operation of holding companies in the United States, were and still are government owned in most European countries; and even where privately owned, as in England and France, they were and still are removed from financial manipulation and stock market speculation to a greater extent than in the United States. Furthermore the object of monopolistic control, which was the moving spirit behind many a holding company in the United States, could at least in most European countries be reached through the organization of cartels. Seldom therefore was the holding company used for the purposes of obtaining monopoly; the Nobel Trust Co., Ltd., and the Reis-und Handels A.-G., a trust of German rice millers, remained isolated phenomena up to the (first) World War." *Encyclopedia of the social sciences*, VII:410, R. Liefmann, "Holding companies—Europe." According to the same source, the most extensive use of the holding company in Europe was to combine companies in different countries (linoleum, soap, silk, petroleum), for patent exploitation, and for finance.

2 A. S. Dewing, Financial policy of corporations. Fourth edition (New York, 1941): 913.

Prior to 1890, authorization to own stock in other corporations was obtained, among others, by the Baltimore and Ohio Railroad (1832), the Pennsylvania Railroad (1850), American Bell Telephone Company (1880), and between 1868 and 1872 by some 40 odd corporations in Pennsylvania. See

In practice the holding company device proved defective as a means of circumventing the Sherman Act. The decision of the Supreme Court in 1904 in the Northern Securities case [193 U.S. 197] disposed of the belief that the holding company was immune to antimonopoly legislation. In 1911 the dismemberment by court decree [221 U.S. 1] of the Standard Oil Company, a holding company, further emphasized this point. Finally, in 1914, the Clayton Act made illegal the acquisition of stock in another company engaged in interstate commerce where the result might be a substantial lessening of competition between the two companies. "Since the passage of the Clayton Act in 1914 the most important single use of the industrial holding company has been in the consolidation of enterprises which were largely non-competing; that is, in the creation of circular or of vertical combinations." [3]

Despite the lessened importance of the holding company as a substantial shield against antimonopoly legislation, other advantages of this method of combination continue to make its use widespread and persistent. For example, it is usually easier to obtain control by means of stock ownership than by means of outright merger or fusion. Furthermore, control may be perpetuated more readily through stock pyramiding. In addition, liability for debts may be restricted to one corporate unit instead of laying the assets of the whole combination open to attack by creditors; change in scale of operations is more easily accomplished when individual corporate units may be created or liquidated at the discretion of a dominant company; the application of an "after-acquired" clause in a mortgage may be avoided by the creation of a separate corporation to hold title to the newly-acquired assets; provisions of state corporation laws hostile to out-of-state corporations may be made inapplicable by incorporation in each state in which business is conducted. This list of uses is by no means exhaustive. New legislation and developments in other fields will continue to create opportunities for the use of a multicorporate combination.[4]

The widespread use of a series of corporations linked together primarily by means of stock ownership brought in its train cer-

---

Encyclopedia of the social sciences, VII:403–9, J. C. Bonbright and G. C. Means, "Holding companies—United States." All of these earlier cases, however, required individual special legislative action. The importance of the New Jersey action lay in the general grant of power to all corporations incorporated in that state.

3 *Encyclopedia of the social sciences*, VII:407, J. C. Bonbright and G. C. Means, "Holding companies—United States."

4 J. C. Bonbright and G. C. Means, Holding companies, (New York, 1932).

tain accounting and legal problems. In the realm of accounting the problem arose of devising statements reflecting the economic unity of the combination without special regard to its legal form; the legal problem became one of reconciling the doctrinal conflicts created by unitary operations through legally separate entities.

Partial Recognition of Entity Transcending Corporate Boundaries

In the nature of the case courts and legislatures move more cautiously than industrialists and accountants in recognizing changes in traditional concepts and modes of behavior. A dynamic world carries with it as an unavoidable consequence a lag behind the changes themselves of the expression in case and statute law of the nature of the altered circumstances. For example, accountants have for years treated the general business partnership as an entity separate and distinct from the partners as individuals. The necessity of separating personal from business affairs is a requirement so well embedded in business and accounting routine that it is rarely stated explicitly. At the same time, only in recent years, in the Uniform Partnership Act, has the law given limited recognition to the partnership as an entity.[5]

A similar recognition by the commercial world, not yet matched by full legal sanction, is present with respect to single proprietorships. The individual as a business unit is not identical with the same individual as a private person. His business affairs, so accounting doctrine insists, must be kept separate from his personal transactions. Consistent with this attitude are the income tax regulations in so far as they treat an individual's business revenues and expenses differently from his personal, nonbusiness receipts and outlays. The standards of conduct, the decisions made, the relationships established in transacting his business affairs differ sufficiently from those applicable to his personal affairs to warrant separate treatment in order to avoid reports at once misleading and distorted.

No general indictment of the law is intended, though at times in specific instances we may wish for quicker legal response to economic stimulus. What is intended is emphasis upon the point that accounting possesses more flexibility than the law—a flexi-

5 For example, under the Uniform Partnership Act partners are agents of the *partnership*, the *partnership* may hold title to property, real and personal, the partners may, in capacities other than as owners, have dealings with the *partnership*, etc.

bility permitting accountants to experiment more freely with new ideas and forms and, by the same token, to reject old ones more readily. Furthermore, once these experiments are past the tentative stage and become well-established and useful, accountants may readily take a hand in shaping the development of the law itself, to stimulate it beyond its own unaided capacity to progress.

Specifically with reference to corporate combination through stock ownership the law has been hesitant and confused; consequently a well-settled consistent body of legal rules and doctrines is not available to resolve the accounting problems in the same field. In 1930, A. A. Berle wrote, "There cannot be said to be a well worked out theory of subsidiary corporations in the present state of the authorities." [6] Despite some advances since Berle wrote, much the same statement may be made today. "The authorities are not completely in accord as to when several corporations will be considered as a single entity. . . . The rule followed in many cases is that the legal fiction of distinct corporate existence may be disregarded where a corporation is so organized and controlled, and its affairs are so conducted, as to make it merely an instrumentality or adjunct of another corporation." [7]

The prevailing legal doctrine is summed up in Majestic Co. v. Orpheum Circuit, Inc. [21 F.2d 720 (C.C.A.Iowa 1927)]:

> In legal conception a corporation has an entity separate and distinct from its stockholders; and the act of the corporation is not that of the stockholders. Nor is its obligation that of its stockholder. . . . A corporation is not liable for the acts or the obligations of another corporation, merely because it controls such other by reason of ownership of its stock. . . . The corporate entity will not be ignored at law nor in equity, whether the control is in the hands of one or many stockholders. . . . The corporation will be regarded as a legal entity as a general rule, and the courts acting cautiously and only when the circumstances justify it, will ignore the fiction of corporate entity, where it is used as a blind or instrumentality to defeat public convenience, justify wrong, or perpetuate a fraud, and will regard the corporation as an association of persons. . . .

Distinctly in the minority, but expressing opinions more consonant with the assumptions made by accountants in preparing consolidated statements, are the decisions and *obiter dicta* in the following cases.

---

6 Cases and materials in the law of corporation finance, (St. Paul, 1930): 809.

7 18 Corpus Juris Secundum: 382–5, "Corporations," Par. 7e.

In 1903, a New Jersey court in a case involving reciprocal stockholdings expressed these views:

And all this most amazing result is reached by construing the enabling act . . . as establishing an absolute and arbitrary right in all corporations to purchase and hold stock in other corporations, and vote thereon, together with the rigid maintenance of the pure fiction of corporate existence, so as to make these fictitious creatures the actual owners of the stock which in equity belongs to their shareholders. . . . The whole scheme is built upon fictions which our law maintains as necessary and valuable for many purposes, but which equity nowadays frequently casts aside for the prevention of fraud and the accomplishment of justice. Robotham v. Prudential Insurance Company, 64 N.J.Eq. 673, 53 Atl. 842.

A decision in a patent suit against a wholly owned subsidiary was held *res judicata* as against the parent on the ground of complete identity of interest. [Hart Steel Co. v. Railroad Supply Co., 244 U.S. 294, 37 S.Ct. 506 (1917)]. In another Supreme Court decision, subsidiary and parent were treated as one with regard to rates. [Chicago, Milwaukee and St. Paul Railway Company v. Minneapolis Civic and Commerce Association, 247 U.S. 490, 38 S.Ct. 553 (1918)].

Emphasis on the reasons for intercorporate shareholdings is evident in the following excerpt:

. . . where such ownership of stock is resorted to, not for the purpose of participating in the affairs of the corporation in which it is held in a manner normal and usual with stockholders, but for the purpose of making it a mere agent, or instrumentality or department of another company, the courts will look through the forms to the realities of the relation between the companies as if the corporate agency did not exist and will deal with them as the justice of the case may require. [U. S. v. Reading Company, 253 U.S. 26, 40 S.Ct. 425 (1920)].

In Industrial Research Corporation v. General Motors Corporation, [29 F.2d 623 (D.C.Ohio 1928)], the court held that ". . . the fiction of corporate entity may be disregarded, where one corporation is so organized and controlled and its affairs are so conducted that it is, in fact, a mere instrumentality or adjunct of another corporation."

A virtually complete break with the concept of the separateness of each corporate entity is expressed by Justice Douglas in a recent case involving the rights of creditors of a subsidiary in the assets of the parent. [Consolidated Rock Products Co. v. du Bois, 312 U.S. 510, 61 S.Ct. 675 (1941)]:

There has been a unified operation of those several properties by Consolidated pursuant to the operating agreement. That operation not only resulted in extensive commingling of assets. All management functions of the several companies were assumed by Consolidated. The subsidiaries abdicated. Consolidated operated them as mere departments of its own business. Not even the formalities of separate corporate organizations were observed, except in minor particulars such as the maintenance of certain separate accounts. In view of these facts, Consolidated is in no position to claim that its assets are insulated from such claims of creditors of the subsidiaries. . . . A holding company which assumes to treat the properties of its subsidiaries as its own cannot take the benefits of direct management without the burdens.

That there has been some recognition of the essential economic unity of a combination held together by stock ownership rather than by fusion or merger seems apparent from the citations given above. Also apparent, however, is the tendency for the courts to view the combination as an entity only under special circumstances and not as a rule or doctrine applicable to the ordinary transactions of a going concern. For example, in Cintas v. American Car and Foundry Co. [131 N.J.Eq. 419, 25 A.2d 418 (1942)], a New Jersey court reviewed the earlier decisions holding combinations to be a unit but decided those cases were all dealing with special points and therefore not binding in a dispute concerning the status of intercompany dividends declared and paid in the ordinary course of business. As a consequence, when preparing the consolidated statements of a group of related corporations, we are dealing with an entity almost wholly, though not entirely, outside the scope of complete legal recognition. Consolidated statements, therefore, need special justification, a condition not required of the statements of a single corporation. Because of the limited status in the eyes of the law of the entities to which they refer consolidated statements must be regarded as auxiliary, special-purpose reports, not primary, all-purpose exhibits supplanting or displacing the statements of legally recognized entities. The nature of the special purposes and auxiliary functions which consolidated statements, in the present state of corporation law, may perform is discussed more fully below.

Development of Use of Consolidated Statements

The history of the development of the use of consolidated statements has been largely the history of the development of the holding company. Although some evidence is available indicating earlier presentation of statements in combined or consolidated form, widespread use did not appear until the first decade of the present century.[8] The United States Steel Corporation, chartered in New Jersey in 1901, presented consolidated statements from its inception. Since then, consolidated financial statements have been a familiar feature of corporate reports.

Aside from the holding company itself, probably the most influential factor in shaping the uneven development of the popularity, the form, and the content of consolidated statements has been the various Federal revenue acts. Although continuous, the intensity of accounting interest in the technical development of these statements seems to vary almost directly with the extent to which consolidated returns are acceptable for income-tax purposes.

From 1917 to 1921, consolidated returns were required of affiliated corporations (as defined in the several acts). The Revenue Act of 1921 placed consolidated returns on an optional basis. A small additional tax for the privilege of filing consolidated returns was imposed in 1932 and 1933. Except for railroads, the privilege was repealed entirely in the 1934 Act. In 1938, street railways were explicitly included in the list of combinations permitted to file consolidated returns; Pan-American trading corporations were added in 1939. For the purposes of the new excess-profits tax, consolidated returns were restored to favor in 1940.[9] Under subsequent revenue acts, affiliated corporations may file consolidated tax returns. If a consolidated return is used, it must be filed for both the income and excess profits taxes, and an additional 2 per cent surtax paid.

The numerous reasons for the changes in attitude of the taxing authorities cannot be explored here. In large part, however, these changes reflect the confusion and inconsistency already noted in the law of intercorporate relations. For example, Article 631 of Regulations 45, relating to the Revenue Act of 1918, stated the case in favor of requiring consolidated returns:

> Otherwise opportunity would be afforded for the evasion of taxation by the shifting of income through price fixing, charges for services, and other means by which income could be arbitrarily assigned to one or another unit of the group. In other cases without a consolidated return excessive taxation might be imposed as a result of purely arti-

---

8 W. Bores, "Geschichtliche Entwicklung der konsolidierten Bilanz" ("Historical development of the consolidated balance sheet", *Zeitschrift für handelswissenschaftliche Forschung*, XXVIII:113–36; 209–22; 327–36.

9 For a concise documented summary of the role of consolidated returns in the Federal tax structure, consult U. S. Temporary National Economic Committee. Investigation of concentration of economic power. Monograph No. 9, C. J. Hynning, "Taxation of corporate enterprise," (Washington, D. C., 1941):41–5.

ficial conditions existing between corporations within a controlled group.

After more than two decades of experience with consolidated returns, the following passage by Hynning was written:

> The holding company and its subsidiaries do not constitute any common unit of responsibility. In the realm of contracts and torts, employees and customers, investors and the general public, corporations are usually allowed to define their duties and liabilities strictly in terms of separate corporate entities, largely irrespective of intercorporate relationships. By defining the "real business unit" on a consolidated basis for affiliated companies, the Federal tax laws accepted a unit of responsibility which was practically non-existent elsewhere in corporate relationships.[10]

Hynning's position is in strict logic probably unsound, but nevertheless quite understandable on psychological grounds. The unsound aspect is the contention that because in most other relationships an affiliated group may take advantage of imperfectly developed legal rules it should be denied recognition of its essential unity in tax matters. The understandable element is the unfavorable reaction to a situation in which affiliated corporations are found claiming to be one and many at the same time, as separate, completely insulated units in arguing a torts case, as mere administrative cells in an organic whole in proceedings concerning tax matters.

In addition to the Bureau of Internal Revenue, other public and quasipublic agencies have given partial or complete recognition to consolidated statements. The California Corporation Law, for example, states that "the balance sheet of a holding corporation may be either its separate balance sheet or a consolidated balance sheet of the holding corporation and its subsidiary corporations." A subsequent provision of the same section, however, requires the separate balance sheet of the holding company as an accompaniment of the consolidated statement.[11]

The Securities and Exchange Commission has discretionary power to require consolidated statements.[12] Up to the present time, however, the Commission has not issued a general regulation making these statements a required part of registration procedure. In practice, nevertheless, most registrants who are parent companies submit consolidated reports, and the Securities and Exchange Commission's Regulation S–X, Article 4, contains direc-

---

[10] Hynning, *op. cit.*, p. 52.

[11] California. Corporations Code. Sec. 3009, as amended, 1949.

[12] Securities Act of 1933. Sec. 19(a). Securities Exchange Act of 1934. Sec. 13(b).

tions as to "consolidated and combined statements" for those electing to use them.

The Department of Stock List of the New York Stock Exchange also provides an option to holding companies of publishing separate statements for the parent and each subsidiary or consolidated statements of the group. For those electing the latter alternative, specific requirements are laid down with respect to the type of information and the amount of detail desired.[13]

Under its financial reporting program the Office of Price Administration permitted a reporting company to file consolidated statements at the company's option, but the Administrator had discretionary power to require consolidated statements in specific cases. When submitted, these statements were in addition to a reporting company's own statements, not substitutes for them.[14]

In England, consolidated statements experienced a slower development than here. Although partially consolidated statements made their appearance earlier, the first publication of fully consolidated reports did not take place until 1934.[15]

The delayed development in England is certainly not the result of legal barriers. At least since 1869 an English corporation could hold the shares of another, unless specifically forbidden by its memorandum or articles of association. [In re Asiatic Banking Corporation, L.R. 4 Ch.App. 252 (1869)]. The Finance (No. 2) Act, 1915, contained provisions permitting the use of consolidated returns in tax matters; the Companies Act, 1929, made the use of consolidated statements permissive for general corporate purposes. The explanation probably lies in the fact that because of the absence of specific antitrust legislation in England, the holding company as known in this country never received as great a stimulus there.

On the Continent, the use of consolidated statements appears even less advanced than in England. Apparently some development occurred after World War I as the result of the "postwar advent of the American banker and investing public into Continental affairs." Some issues floated in New York had consol-

---

13 Accountants' handbook. Third edition. (New York, 1943):1066.

14 Office of Price Administration. Instruction book (revised December 1, 1942) for filing Form A—Annual financial report and Form B—Interim financial report. (Washington, D.C., 1943)

15 Dunlop Rubber Co., Ltd. See the May 12, 1934 issue of *The accountant* (London), XC:651–2, 676–9, for a copy and discussion of these statements. Examples of earlier fragmentary consolidations are cited by Wm. Cash, "Consolidated balance sheets," *The accountant*, LXXXI:726 (December 7, 1929).

idated statements as one of the requirements of the trust indenture.[16]

In brief, consolidated statements are indigenous to American financial reporting. The special form taken by the combination movement in the United States appears to account adequately for this behavior. In some small measure the device found its way to Europe, in part as a response to similar conditions there, in part as an incidental by-product of the export of American capital in the early 1920s. Even in this country, paralleling an incomplete and inadequate comprehension of the essential economic unity of a combination through stock ownership, consolidated statements have not been generally accepted by the courts as replacements of "legal-entity" reports. Their status remains that of a supplement, a complement, an addition to but not a substitute for the statements of individual corporate units. This position is reflected in the rule sometimes encountered that consolidated statements should not be presented in isolation from the individual reports of a parent company and its major subsidiaries. For example take the following passage by E. L. Kohler:

> Combined financial statements portray the joint position or operating results of two or more business or other units as though but one existed. *They are secondary rather than primary in character,* and, as enlargements of the financial statements of a common controlling interest, they assist in explaining the relationships of that interest to the outside world.[17]

When, if ever, the principal legal unit becomes the combination as a whole, this rule will need revision, consolidated statements will become primary in character, and the statements of constituent units will be relegated to a status approximating that now held by departmental operating schedules.

Quantitative Importance of Holding Company In United States

In 1938, according to the Securities and Exchange Commission, 58 per cent of registered corporations had at least one subsidiary.[18] The parent-subsidiary relationship was found in every

16 *The accountant* (London), LXXXII:20, (Jan. 4, 1930).

17 "Some tentative propositions underlying consolidated reports," *Accounting review*, XIII:63 (March, 1938). Italics are added.

18 Quantitative data cited in this section are taken from United States Securities and Exchange Commission, Statistics of American listed corporations. Part I (December, 1940). The statistics cover 1,961 corporations reg-

important industrial group in the economy. The average number of active subsidiaries per registrant was 10.1. More than 20 per cent of all subsidiaries were incorporated abroad.

Except for the electric light and power industry, 70 per cent of all domestic active subsidiaries were one step removed from their parents, that is, direct subsidiaries. Twenty-three per cent were two steps removed, 5 per cent three steps, and 2 per cent four or more steps from the parent company. In the electric light and power industry, the percentage of indirectly controlled subsidiaries is somewhat higher. With respect to percentage of control, over four-fifths of the subsidiaries were controlled by their immediate parents through ownership of at least 95 per cent of their voting power.

It may therefore be concluded that, for the important segment of American business represented by the Securities and Exchange Commission's summary, (1) the type of intercorporate relationship giving rise to the use of consolidated statements is prevalent in all sectors of the economy, (2) foreign subsidiaries play a significant part in the American corporate structure, (3) subholding companies are employed extensively enough to warrant some attention, and (4) the problem of outside or minority interest is of strategic importance in about one-fifth of the cases.

---

istered as of June 30, 1938, under the Securities Exchange Act of 1934. The included corporations possessed between 50 and 60 per cent of the total assets of the corresponding industrial groups.

II

BASIC PREMISES

UNDERLYING the subsequent discussion and serving as a foundation upon which it rests are certain basic premises with respect to the problem at issue. The first two premises, namely, the essential economic unity of a holding company group, and the auxiliary nature of consolidated statements, are discussed together and are derived from the considerations presented in the preceding chapter. The last four, the primacy of proper asset valuation, adherence to conventional accounting rules and standards, adherence to the concept of a going-concern, and the desirability of consistency, are derived from concepts common to the body of general accounting doctrine.

Based upon the historical development of the holding company-subsidiary relationship and upon the functions performed by consolidation through share ownership, the position is taken that we are dealing with an economic or business entity composed of legally-separate units subject to a common control based primarily upon powers conferred by share ownership. A similar reliance upon historical developments in the legal field leads to the proposition that consolidated statements, at the present time, must be considered as adjuncts of the legal statements of the parent company and its subsidiaries. Consolidation through stockholdings performs functions similar to consolidation through merger or fusion; consequently consolidated statements should reflect the status and operations of the affiliated group as though it were fused in the legal as well as the economic sense. At the same time certain legal relationships, for example, creditors' rights and dividend limits, will probably be determined on the basis of existing legal entities; consequently the statements of each legal entity involved may not be discarded as superficial or redundant. As a matter of fact, since the courts in enforcing their decisions may apply sanctions not available to other agencies their prescriptions must be conformed with, even though demonstrably incorrect. Though a revision in the prevailing law of intercorporate relationships may be desirable, consolidated statements must still be treated as auxiliary, not primary.

In the light of this enforced secondary role, to what groups or interests will consolidated statements prove useful? Despite the decision in the Consolidated Rock Products Case [312 U.S. 510, 61 S.Ct. 675 (1941)], almost certainly not to the creditors of a subsidiary corporation. In the absence of intercompany guaranties of debt payment, creditors must look for payment, as a general rule, to the assets of the debtor corporation and not to its stockholders, corporate or otherwise. As a result the statements of interest to creditors of subsidiaries are those of the specific legal entity against which their claims run.

In general, presumably, outside or minority stockholders of subsidiaries will not receive any information of direct benefit to them from consolidated reports. As consolidated groups function the outside shareholders are mere passive participants in the combination. The fate of their investment is almost completely at the mercy of the controlling group. This is not meant in any sense invidious to the group in control but in the simple and obvious sense that in matters of business policy the outside shareholders must accept the decisions of the controlling group. The participation by outsiders may be profitable to them—their anticipations probably run along these lines—but nevertheless they are in no position, legally or economically, to direct the ordinary course of business events impinging on their investments. To these shareholders the statements of immediate direct interest are those of the legal entity whose stocks they own.[1]

The short-term creditors of a dominant company are apparently in the same position with respect to consolidated reports as the creditors and shareholders of subsidiaries. The liquid assets out of which they may look for payment, and, if need be, against which they may enforce payment through appropriate court action, are those of the dominant company itself. A dominant company may itself possess and use the power to appropriate the liquid assets of subsidiaries through borrowings and dictated dividends but the short-term creditors have no legal right to insist that a dominant company "milk" a subsidiary for their benefit. The claims run against a single legal entity, the parent; the parent's statements then are the ones to be obtained and analyzed.

In the general case in which special provisions giving them a lien on subsidiaries' assets are absent, long-term creditors of the dominant company may obtain some useful information from

[1] The position taken here should be modified to allow for the fact that a collapse of the consolidation may involve the subsidiary and its outside shareholders. A series of consolidated statements may indicate a marked trend toward financial disaster, thereby warning minority as well as controlling shareholders of impending difficulties. Similarly, creditors of a relatively weak subsidiary may assume that a strong well-financed dominant company will extend aid to its affiliates. If this assumption is at all warranted in a specific instance, consolidated reports will prove of some use to those without direct legal claims against the dominant company or the group.

consolidated reports concerning the probable future trend of a dominant company's assets, although indications of this nature will be highly tentative. The potential usefulness of consolidated statements in this connection should not be minimized or overlooked, but it is hardly sufficient to justify their preparation and use as a matter of accounting routine.

A discussion of the use that regulatory commissions may make of consolidated statements cannot be undertaken here. In general, however, it appears that regulatory bodies are more interested in proper accounting for individual inter-company transactions than in accounting for the group of controlled companies as a whole. For example, the problem of determining a rate base for an operating utility which is also a subsidiary is in part a problem of determining the reasonableness of charges incurred on intercompany transactions. In addition, to inhibit acts contrary to public policy or detrimental to the interests of investors and creditors (a problem created by any type of highly concentrated control over a wide area) may be more difficult if the abuses are screened by the interposition of numerous legal entities. In this type of situation governmental agencies will be more likely to require detailed information concerning specific aspects of intercompany relationships than general over-all data depicting the combination as a unit, with intercompany relationships erased or submerged.[2]

Two groups, the management and the stockholders of a dominant company, remain as the ones to whom consolidated statements tend to overshadow single-company reports in importance. Investment in a dominant company is an investment in the entire affiliated group. Information concerning the entire area of investment is consequently of prime importance to investors. To an even greater extent is it of importance to management.

As the agency in direct control of the affairs of the combination management must have data concerning its functioning. Information of this nature will be obtained from many sources; but the major source of the type of data expressible in financial terms is a set of consolidated statements of the group as a whole. To management these statements tend to appear as primary in character; statements of the operations of constituent units then fulfill the function of schedules supporting the principal generalized presentation. As a matter of business policy the

[2] For example the Public Utility Holding Company Act of 1935 prohibits numerous intercompany practices and the Securities and Exchange Commission in administering the Act requires conformance to specified standards in accounts reflecting intercompany transactions.

statements of individual units may not, of course, be neglected; neither may the reports of individual plants and branch offices in a large single-corporate enterprise. Commitments difficult of revision may be made with respect to allocation of resources and of personnel to various sections of the concern, but such problems are characteristic of all large-scale operations, not merely of combinations through share ownership. The essential feature of these combinations, as with all combinations, is central direction and control. Reports and statements relating to the field of direct control are logical concomitants of this feature.

To what extent stockholders are really informed by means of conventional reports is a question pertinent to the whole field of corporate accounting practices. In accordance, however, with the canon that present and prospective shareholders are entitled to a full report on their field of investment, regardless of the use they may make of the data, it is concluded that consolidated statements are essential components of a complete accounting. From a long-range point of view a consolidated report is undoubtedly superior to a statement of the dominant company taken alone. Over a period of years, the value of the stock and the dividend policy of the top parent company will correlate closely with the progress of the entire group.

In terms of the immediate future, however, investors will probably find a dominant company's legal statements more informative. This is particularly true where share prices are highly speculative, and inordinately influenced by the outlook for the immediate future. The most important single feature in gauging immediate prospects appears to be the likelihood of early dividends. With respect to dividends a dominant company must apparently be guided by a narrow legalistic approach. As a consequence of decisions such as the recent one in the American Car and Foundry Case dividends must presumably be based on the holding company itself viewed as a distinct separate entity [Cintas v. American Car and Foundry Co., 131 N.J.Eq. 419, 25 A.2d 418 (1942)]. In this case all subsidiaries were completely owned within the affiliated group, the officers and directors of constituent companies were for the most part the same individuals, the main offices of each unit were at the same address, and the books of account were kept by a central auditing unit, although separate records were maintained for each corporation. The dominant company had based its dividend policy on consolidated net income but the court overruled it. ". . . the defendant company must be considered a separate and distinct entity for the purpose of fixing dividends and the earning and profits of the subsidiary companies do not enure to the benefit of defendant's stockholders until dividends are actually declared by its subsidiaries."

Alternative conceptions of the nature of consolidated statements will not bear rigorous analysis. The most plausible of the alternatives conceives of consolidated statements as mere statistical exhibits of selected financial data relating to a unified group of companies. This approach is attractive as a means of avoiding a head-on conflict with the hesitancy of legal doctrine to recognize the essential unity of a consolidated group. If this compromise is adopted, however, too much is sacrificed. Modern accounting, imperfect as it may be as a projection of economic position, possesses extremely valuable mechanical features not to be lightly discarded. The necessity of operating within the framework of the fundamental accounting equation imposes the condition of considering all pertinent phases of enterprise operations. For example, a change in assets may not be reflected without considering and recording the effect on other elements of the accounting equation. No such rigorous formal standard serves as a guide in preparing a statistical exhibit of, let us say, inventories held by affiliated companies. A further consideration against the statistical conception lies in the fact that modern accounting analysis requires an entity in terms of which economic and business events may be examined. The entity may be legal or economic, actual or proposed, real or imaginary, but once defined the strengths and safeguards of double-entry bookkeeping should be employed.

No objections may be made, of course, to the use of statistical exhibits as supplements or notes to financial statements. The status of properties in war zones, for example, is highly uncertain. Assuredly no justification exists for merging their accounts with assets not so situated, yet their existence should be indicated. One reasonable solution of the dilemma is to exclude them from the body of the reports but to describe their latest known status in a supplementary schedule.

The partnership concept may possibly be invoked as a basis on which to construct consolidated statements. This alternative may assume two forms: first, the statements are based upon a presumed partnership of corporations, or second, they reflect a presumed partnership of controlling and outside interests. The first form assumes that the constituent companies are on a plane of rough equality, an assumption not consistent with the actual functioning of a holding company group. Fundamentally the same objection may be made to the second form. No partnership in any but the most strained sense exists between controlling and outside interests. True, a minority interest in a subsidiary has rights which must be respected but this consideration acts merely as a limit to the freedom of action of the controlling group. The minority may not act independently or exercise veto power over business policy determined by a controlling interest.

Consolidated statements, then, are primarily of interest to the management and stockholders of a dominant company. Other groups may on occasion find incidental use for them but not as essential primary reports. As a result the preparation of consolidated statements resolves itself into a problem in the preparation of statements useful to a dominant company's management and stockholders in obtaining a report on the concern as a whole.

The four remaining premises to which explicit reference is made all stem from considerations present in most problems of modern accounting. They do not depend for their validity and usefulness on any special features of consolidation. They are sufficiently important for purposes of the subsequent discussion, however, to warrant specific recognition and elaboration at this point.

The primacy of proper asset valuation derives directly from basic attributes of the fundamental accounting process. The accounting equation, either in the form A minus L equals P, or A equals L plus P, demands that we work from assets and debts to the proprietary equity. Proprietary equity is equal to the difference between the values assigned to assets and the values assigned to debts. This holds true for the enterprise taken as a whole as well as for individual transactions in which it may participate. In other words, the values assigned to the proprietary accounts are dependent for their magnitude upon values assigned to assets and debts, and the principal independent variable in the equation is the value of total assets. This underlying conception of the whole process of rational bookkeeping is merely a formal reflection of the fact that an enterprise derives value for its owners through actual and prospective favorable changes in assets under its control. Regardless of what may be done in certain quarters, we find untenable, for example, the practice of first assigning a value to capital stock and then creating asset categories of equal amount. Practices of this type strip the rational element from the bookkeeping process and make of it simply a handmaiden of those who wish to "prove" a predetermined result.

The principal problem, then, from a strictly logical point of view, is the determination of appropriate values for assets. Given those values, the size of the proprietary equity is determined simply by deducting the amount of creditor claims or debts. Of course, the problem is rarely exhausted with the calculation of the magnitude of the proprietary equity or changes therein. The further problems of assigning the changes to the proper accounting period and to the several ownership interests will remain—problems by no means easy or obvious of solution. Nevertheless, preëminently and necessarily the soundness and completeness of the treatment accorded assets are of concern before the problems associated with equities may logically be examined.

The application of this premise to specific problems of consolidation is deferred for later more detailed consideration. At this point, however, it may be pointed out that in preparing a consolidated statement the temptation must be resisted to use assets as balancing figures to offset magnitudes already assigned to equities.

Insofar as possible the rules and conventional procedures prevalent in accounting for a single corporation will be applied. For example, the rule will be invoked that fixed assets are to be recorded at cost or other acquisition value, less depreciation. Any deviation must then be justified on the basis of special considerations present in consolidation but absent in other situations. Reliance on this premise is a methodological choice, not a conviction. This must be so because the bald statement of the premise implies the existence of an established body of universally accepted "rules and procedures prevalent in accounting for a single corporation," a condition which decidedly does not exist. As a result, where competing rules are present, reference will be made to the one which seems most widely adopted or most reasonable. Controversies over issues not germane to consolidated accounts are thereby avoided. Attention will then be centered on the subject at hand; he who holds to some other "prevalent rule" is free to make the requisite modification in the discussion without the necessity of rearguing the whole case as it relates to consolidation. Clearly, then, unless the context specifically so indicates, citation of a particular accounting standard does not imply approval.

The concept of a going concern is so much a part of the theoretical backbone of modern accounting as to require no extended comment. Its application to consolidation implies that the situations envisaged in the discussion are not those of companies in process of dissolution or disintegration. Except for precise, definite indications to the contrary, a consolidated group is presumed to continue into the indefinite future as a functioning entity. Special problems surrounding liquidation or fundamental reorganization of a combination are therefore largely excluded. Except for the reorganizations inherent in the administration of the Public Utility Holding Company Act of 1935, explicit reference to this premise would be superfluous. Lest anyone be tempted to interpret this study in the light of the problems raised by that Act, it is here stated specifically that a discussion of those special problems is in the main not within the scope of this study nor the competence of the author. Problems of public policy, of technical industrial organization, and of corporate financial practices are involved which a formal accounting treatment is certainly helpless to resolve and probably unable to clarify in any significant sense.

Because of the uncertainty to which most accounting calculations are subject, consistency of treatment from period to period is desirable as a means of obtaining statistical comparability. Bias or omissions will thereby in all probability be similar from year to year so that direction of change will be reflected even though absolute measures may be defective. Complete accuracy is, of course, the ideal goal and is to be reflected whenever possible. But accuracy depends upon adequate knowledge and foresight, conditions unfortunately absent in many important circumstances. As a consequence, to save accounting records from becoming mere reflections of highly subjective personal judgments and prepossessions, reliance is placed on certain objective rules and standards which will at least serve to make accounting procedures coherent.

Consistency, in the sense of adherence to established rules of measurement and interpretation, must not, however, become a fetish, a blind, obstinate opposition to necessary alterations. When consolidated goodwill, for example, is included as the result of a conventional disposition of an excess of the nominal value of shares issued over book value of equity acquired, it is undesirable to continue reflecting that item in subsequent statements in the face of an operating history clearly disposing of the last vestige of evidence of superior or differential earning power. The accounting rule relating to consolidated goodwill is useful when only surmises concerning future developments are at hand; after experience has yielded knowledge, the rule is a positive barrier to proper accounting. Somewhere between the ideal of complete accuracy and the human desire to cling to definite formulas a rational basis on which to work must be found.

III

THE AREA OF CONSOLIDATION

THE PRESENTATION of consolidated statements is in order whenever there exists an economic or business entity composed of two or more legal units. Conversely, consolidated statements will not be prepared when an economic entity does not exist. The general principle is clear, almost self-evident. In many cases, perhaps the majority, its application is easy. For example, a group of corporations, formerly branches of the present parent company, all engaged in the same type of business in the same geographical area, and all of whose shares are entirely owned by the parent, constitutes an easily identifiable business entity, and consolidated statements are clearly in order. On the other hand no entity is discernible when a bank acting as trustee holds title to a majority of shares in several corporations not otherwise related. In cases of this type no one would recommend consolidation of accounts.

In other situations, however, the principle is far from easy of application. Consequently, concrete form must be given to the general principle in order to make it objective and definite. For example, the Securities and Exchange Commission states in its Accounting Series Release No. 32:

> The specific principles followed should be objective and definite, such as, for example, that the registrant includes in consolidation all wholly-owned subsidiaries, or all domestic wholly-owned subsidiaries or all wholly-owned manufacturing subsidiaries.

The need for explicitly stated objective standards arises from the wide circulation accorded published statements. So long as statements are prepared for private circulation and use, this consideration is largely inoperative. The desired area of consolidation will in that case be indicated; an accountant then merely uses his technical skill to give expression to the intended result. The reports are tailor-made, cut to a customer's specific pattern. As soon, however, as the statements are given general circulation their specific frame of reference must either be known to potential users or clearly expressed in the statements themselves, otherwise the data presented may be variously interpreted or misunderstood.

Numerous criteria have been employed for the determination of the area of consolidation. Attention will be directed to the leading ones in an attempt to develop a useful set of guides consistent with the major goal of consolidation.

Percentage of Stock Ownership as a Standard

Obviously, consolidation through share ownership cannot exist without the concentration of subsidiaries' shares in the hands of a dominant company. Consequently it is not surprising to find percentage of stock ownership cited frequently as the appropriate standard to use. The emphasis properly belongs, however, not only on the ownership of the shares but on the power that ownership confers. The necessary condition for unified operation of a group of corporations is centralized control. Control is most easily centralized by domination of the board of directors of each company; and this domination is most readily and firmly secured by possession and exercise of the votes needed to elect the board. One important outward manifestation, in other words, of the existence of control is the ownership of voting shares. The error must be avoided, however, of confusing the reflection with the object, of identifying share ownership with control. Control, it should be emphasized, is the strategic element and it is on control that attention should be centered.

But a difficulty is immediately apparent. "Control" as such lacks objective manifestations, a condition which the formulation of standards should seek to remedy. Possession and exercise of the power to dominate a board of directors is most easily recognized by the ownership of voting shares and the use of the accompanying voting power to control another company's operations. Consequently, as a determinant of a parent-subsidiary relationship majority ownership of voting stock is a useful test.

A clear-cut example of complete ownership and control was that of St. Louis Car Company which owned all the authorized stock of two subsidiaries.[1] A borderline case was presented by the Armco International Corporation which owned, indirectly, a bare 50 per cent of a subsidiary's voting securities but, by virtue of a contract with other shareholders, was entitled to nominate a majority of the Board of Directors.[2] In the former case the existence of complete ownership of all voting stock establishes the fact of control; in the latter case, knowledge of the percentage of ownership is insufficient, taken by itself, to reveal the relationship.

---

1 Securities and exchange commission. Survey of American listed corporations. Report No. 7, "Railroad equipment," p. 9, notes 4 and 5.

2 *Ibid.* Report No. 6, "Steel producers," p. 17, n. 3.

When, as frequently happens, nonvoting shares exist, a further complication is introduced. Ownership of a controlling majority of voting shares is, in those cases, not synonymous with majority ownership of proprietary equity. As long as the nonvoting securities remain without franchise no new problem is raised; securities with that characteristic may be treated as bonds with indefinite maturities and interest rates. Many types of "nonvoting" securities, however, possess contingent voting rights; for example, a preferred issue may acquire full voting rights if dividends are not paid for a specified length of time. As a consequence, when the contingency becomes actual, a dominant company in possession of a majority of shares ordinarily carrying full voting power, but without majority ownership of other classes of securities, may find itself ousted from control. In other words, continuous control through stock ownership may not even be reasonably secure unless a clear-cut majority of all securities with actual or potential voting power is owned. Therefore, even when an overwhelming majority of voting shares is owned, consideration must be given to a potential break-up of the combination through a shift in voting power. Until the shift takes place, however, there is no effect on the area of consolidation.

Aside from the possible complications introduced by several classes of stock majority ownership is not always associated with active immediate control because, for example, "ownership is temporary, strong individuals constitute an effective, satisfactory management, or . . . contractual relationship with a creditor or other outsider substantially limits the possibility of control through stock ownership. Such companies can be referred to as 'uncontrolled'." [3] The existence of the last condition mentioned by Kohler definitely destroys the centralized control necessary for consolidation. On the basis of the going-concern premise, the first condition, that of temporary control, is likewise destructive of the necessary unity. Lack of intention to incorporate the temporarily-controlled unit into the combination is necessary, of course, as the basis of its treatment as "uncontrolled," but that meaning seems implicit in the quoted statement. But the second condition, the existence of effective, satisfactory management, is not entirely acceptable as a reason for exclusion from consolidation. As long as the management in question follows policies consistent with the views of the controlling interest, such management may be considered a part of the com-

[3] E. L. Kohler, "Some tentative propositions underlying consolidated reports," *Accounting review*, XIII:64 (March, 1938).

bination. Failure to act in that manner will undoubtedly result in the installation of a new management. Merely because a dominant company refrains from placing its own specifically-chosen nominees in charge of a subsidiary's operations does not remove that company from the area of consolidation.

In general, claims that undoubted majority ownership is not associated with control should be viewed with suspicion. Disavowal of control over subsidiaries may be made for the sake of expediency in strengthening a dominant company's case before a regulatory commission or for other opportunistic purposes. For example, on its face the denial by Pullman Incorporated of "the power to direct or cause the direction of the management and policies" of certain subsidiaries was weak. In six of the subsidiaries in question, the Company owned 100 per cent of the stock; in three others, 99.9 per cent, 99.69 per cent, and 96.67 per cent, respectively.[4]

An example of majority ownership without clear-cut control is offered by the case of an oil company which owned, directly and indirectly, 65 per cent of the outstanding shares of a subsidiary but, under terms of a voting trust agreement was entitled to appoint only two of the four voting trustees. In a situation of this type recourse must be had to other data, particularly with respect to the affiliations of the other two voting trustees, before a decision may be reached regarding the existence of centralized control.[5]

More numerous and usually more difficult to deal with are the cases in which active control is associated with minority ownership. For convenience those situations are included in this category in which a dominant company holds in its own name a minority of a subsidiary's shares but actually is in a position to vote a majority. For example, Company P owns 100 per cent of the stock of Company S and 20 per cent of Company T's stock, while Company S owns the remaining 80 per cent of T's shares. Complete ownership is obviously held within the affiliation. Closely allied in effect to cases of indirect ownership are those in which large individual stockholders of a subsidiary are also owners of shares in a parent company and vote with it to con-

4 Securities and exchange commission. Survey of American listed corporations. Report No. 7, "Railroad equipment," p. 9, note 3.

5 *ibid.* Report No. 1, "Oil refining," p. 29, note 21.

trol the subsidiary. Kohler summarizes this general type of control in the following concise form:

> Ownership of voting stock by subsidiaries, directors, officers, employees, nominees, or other persons having subordinated interests.[6]

Since in each such instance unified control is presumably present, consolidation is clearly in order despite the apparent absence of majority ownership.

An extreme example of complete control without ownership interest of any magnitude was afforded by the relationship between Bethlehem Steel Company (Pa.) and Cambria Iron Company. Bethlehem owned none of the outstanding capital stock of Cambria but leased all its properties under a 999-year lease. "The accounts of Cambria Iron Company are included in the consolidated statements and schedules . . ., except that in each case the par value of the outstanding stock of Cambria Iron Company owned by the public is treated as an indebtedness of one of the subsidiaries consolidated and the rental paid under the Cambria Lease is deducted in determining the consolidated net income." [7]

In the types of "minority" ownership cited thus far, no real problem exists provided the facts are known. In each case what appeared to be less than majority ownership turned out on closer inspection to be virtually complete ownership. The exact voting strength may be obscured by indirect ownership, voting trusts, nominees, shares in the names of directors, and the like, but once these facts are known the existence of control becomes clear and preparation of consolidated statements is justified.

What of the situations in which *bona fide* minority ownership exists, not convertible into a majority by nominees and voting trusts? Are consolidated statements to be prepared when a parent company lacks even a bare majority of the equity allotted to the voting shareholders? The issue raised is essentially one of deciding the relative weights to be assigned to "stock ownership" and "centralized control" as determinants of the existence of a combination. For example, the charter of the Des

[6] Kohler, *op. cit.*, p. 64.

"All of the stock of this company stands in the name of a director of the registrant, and he has given a declaration of trust with reference thereto in favor of the registrant. Of record the voting rights are in the name of said director but they are in fact exercised by him as trustee for the registrant and under its direction." Securities and exchange commission. Survey of American listed corporations. Report No. 8, "General industrial machinery," p. 12, note 3.

[7] Securities and exchange commission. Survey of American listed corporations. Report No. 6, "Steel producers," p. 18, note 6.

Moines Union Railway Company provided that no director could be elected, no amendments to the articles adopted, and no increase in capital stock voted except by a seven-eighths vote of the voting stock.[8] As a consequence, once entrenched, a group with one share over one-eighth of the voting stock could remain in control indefinitely. Suppose that a similar provision existed in a subsidiary's charter and that a parent company originally held a clear majority of voting stock but had gradually divested itself of all but the necessary controlling shares, meanwhile dominating the subsidiary completely. In an instance of this nature, is the subsidiary to be treated as "uncontrolled"? Clearly the area of consolidation has not altered. Centralized control still exists despite the relative smallness of the dominant company's equity, and use of consolidated statements is still appropriate.

Consideration of this special type of case serves to emphasize the point that effective control is the decisive factor; stock ownership is merely the instrumentality by means of which control is maintained.

Less easy of solution are the cases in which active control is associated with minority ownership, not as the result of special charter provisions or other contractual devices but as the result of an apathetic, passive, or satisfied majority. It is a commonplace of corporation finance that control of a corporation with widely dispersed share ownership may usually be obtained by a single person or unified group holding only a fraction of the total voting strength. With widespread diffusion of a majority of the shares an energetic single-minded minority group finds it relatively easy to obtain and keep domination of the board of directors. Where only about 50 per cent of the voting privileges attaching to outstanding shares were ever exercised, ownership by a parent company of 28 per cent of the outstanding shares was sufficient to give it control over the board and policies of the subsidiary.[9] A similar situation evidently exists in numerous other cases. United Chemicals, Inc., for example, owned 27.5 per cent of the voting stock of Westvaco Chlorine Products Corporation. However, "five directors, four of whom are also officers (of United Chemicals) constitute a majority of the Board of Directors of the Westvaco Chlorine Products Corporation,

---

[8] Cited in C. W. Gerstenberg and W. S. Johnson, Organization and Control, (New York, 1917), ch. xviii.

[9] Inspiration Consolidated Copper Company Registration Statement, SEC File 2–4235–1–1. The case is summarized in *Accounting review*, XV:261–5, (June, 1940).

and with one exception are also officers of that company."[10] Union Oil Company of California reported minority ownership of voting stock accompanied by majority representation on the Board of Directors of Outer Harbor Dock and Wharf Company (California).[11]

By way of contrast, however, Electric Time Company, Inc. (Boston) was excluded from consolidation with Warren Telechron Company and General Electric Company despite the existence of actual control by virtue of majority representation on the Board of Directors. Through Warren Telechron, General Electric had a 43.75 per cent interest in Electric Time Company but the immediate parent, Warren Telechron, held a bare 50 per cent of its voting stock.[12]

The difficulty in cases of this nature lies in the fact that control is contingent upon continued apathy of the majority shareholders or their continued satisfaction with the way the company is being managed. Potentially the unorganized majority possesses the power to seize control, thereby removing one unit from the combination. Moreover if continuance of the minority group in active control is dependent upon satisfaction with or confidence in the policies of this group on the part of the majority, an adequate justification for consolidation of reports is clearly lacking; in this situation those in immediate control are in effect the representatives of the stockholders holding a majority of the voting power.

Where the available data are such as to satisfy the accountant that a minority holding carries with it complete domination of the board of directors, and the continuing power to carry into action the policies of the minority group, centralization of control exists and consolidation of accounts is proper. In the absence of indications of this nature, however, the conclusion is justified that no entity exists which can be properly reflected through consolidated statements.

Objection may be raised that adoption of this conclusion would lead to the preparation of statements in which the controlling interest has less than half of the equity in consolidated capital. But failure to meet this test should be no bar to consolidation. The essential objective of consolidated statements is to present an accounting projection of the combination as a whole—all its

---

10 Securities and exchange commission. Survey of American listed corporations. Report No. 2, "Chemicals—fertilizers," p. 18, note 10.

11 *Ibid.*, Report No. 1, "Oil Refining," p. 31, note 29.

12 *Ibid.*, Report No. 10, "Electrical supplies and equipment other than household appliances," p. 13, note 3.

assets and all its debts, as well as its earnings. To whom the earnings accrue and what groups possess an interest in the combination are then reflected in the distribution of consolidated net income and the allocation of consolidated capital. The management of a dominant company is still in need of information concerning the position and functioning of the group as a unit. The stockholders comprising the controlling interest still need data regarding the combination in order to chart the probable long-term trend of their investment. The relative smallness of their interest compared with total consolidated capital merely decreases the percentage of future benefits of the combination to which they may look forward.

In brief, percentage of stock ownership is not in itself satisfactory as a standard indicating the precise extent of the area of consolidation. Except for somewhat arbitrary boundaries which may prove useful for purposes of regulation, taxation, and the like, no general quantitative formulation may be made which will equate the essential factor, control, with the amount of a parent's stock interest in its subsidiaries. Even if the possibilities created by several classes of stock are waived by conceding actual or potential voting rights to all shares, majority holdings without control are known to exist and, more commonly, minority holdings with control. Rules of thumb may be formulated but in the nature of the case they cannot become universal standards. The presence or absence of control must be smoked out by whatever means possible, including a careful consideration of the relationships and their implications created by share ownership. In each situation, then, it is incumbent upon accountants, as a part of the preparation of consolidated statements, to describe carefully the tests employed to establish centralized control, the essential condition calling for presentation of this type of statement.

"Controlling Influence" as a Standard

A distinction must be maintained between broad rules designed to cover virtually all possible cases of a parent-subsidiary relationship, and a standard of accounting procedure. A rule of the former type is useful as a first approximation; it aids in defining the boundaries within which we may reasonably expect to find the business entities sought. A rule of the latter type is an injunction to proceed beyond a mere survey or examination of the field to the preparation and presentation of a relatively precise description, in accounting terms, of the well-defined entities discovered.

Bonbright and Means, for example, offer the following definition:

> A holding company may then be defined in terms of its distinguishing characteristic as any company with share capital which is *in a position to control or materially to influence* the management of one or more other companies by virtue, in part at least, of its ownership of securities of the latter.[13]

As a guide to a study in corporation finance or the economics of intercorporate relationships the definition quoted is useful. By carefully surveying the field for corporations with the indicated characteristics, no one is likely to overlook any important instance of a combination through stock ownership. In the course of the survey, however, he will also, in all likelihood, examine many cases in which these characteristics are present but which on closer examination prove to be outside the scope of the intended area of study. An investment trust may be "in a position to control or materially to influence" other companies, but if it does not exercise that influence no business entity exists. Likewise an investment banker may be temporarily in a similar position but again the centralized control essential to call forth consolidated statements is absent. As an accounting standard, therefore, the definition cited and others similar in tone are not adequate.

In the Public Utility Holding Company Act of 1935 a statutory *prima facie* test of control is provided. All companies in the designated categories owning more than 10 per cent of the voting securities of another company are presumed to possess a "controlling influence" over the other company and must register with the Securities and Exchange Commission.[14] The manifest purpose of the statutory test is to insure full compliance with the intent of the Act. The flexibility necessary to the proper administration of the statute is provided by the discretion accorded the Commission to determine whether registrants under the Act must reorganize. The 10 per cent rule is useful as a device to implement legislative intent; as a prescription for locating definitely a holding company group it is defective because the emphasis is on "controlling influence," not on the actual exercise of control.

In another connection the limitation under discussion is recognized by the Securities and Exchange Commission itself as an

13 Encyclopedia of the social sciences, VII:403–4, J. C. Bonbright and G. C. Means, "Holding companies—United States." Italics added.

14 A full discussion of this aspect of the Act is found in 8 S. E. C. 326. In the matter of Cities Service Company.

inappropriate accounting rule. Regulation S-X provides for inclusion in consolidated statements of "majority-owned subsidiaries" only, a term which embraces companies whose voting shares are more than 50 per cent owned by a parent.[15] The 50 per cent rule itself may be accepted merely as a crude but perhaps convenient rule of thumb; nevertheless the existence of the rule emphasizes the distinction between registration as a *possible* holding company, on the one hand, and treatment as a holding company in published statements and reports on the other. "Controlling influence" must be rejected as a guide; the influence must be actual, not merely potential.

Similarity of Operations as a Standard

In a group of affiliated companies a conflict may be present between similarity of general objectives and dissimilarity of the means employed. The combination presumably exists for the purpose of strengthening the financial position and earning power of the group in control; to this extent, regardless of the types of operations conducted within the combination, the objectives are similar. The constituent units may be engaged in activities of such disparate nature, however, that a real doubt is cast upon the advisability of consolidating accounts. For example, on December 31, 1941, Pullman, Incorporated, through 100 per cent control of Pullman-Standard Car Manufacturing Company, held 96.67 per cent control of Pullman Trust and Savings Bank.[16] On the same date Bethlehem Steel Corporation owned 100 per cent of the voting stock of Farmers' and Merchants' Bank.[17]

Unquestionably the banks are part of the consolidated group subject to centralized control; the investments in the banks, it may be presumed, are on the whole profitable to the parent companies and consequently will be continued. Despite these considerations the exclusion of these companies from consolidation seems eminently proper. Operations of a purely financial nature, such as those of a bank or insurance company, are so different from operations in the extractive industries, in manufacturing, or in trading activities as to call for separate treatment. To combine

15 Article 4, relating to consolidated and combined statements.

16 Securities and exchange commission. Survey of American listed corporations. Report no. 7, "Railroad equipment," p. 7. The Bank's accounts were not consolidated with Pullman's.

17 *Ibid.*, Report no. 6, "Steel producers," p. 9. The Bank's accounts were excluded from consolidation, but included were those of a water company, a transportation company, a light, heat, and fuel company, and a steamship company, in addition to steel fabricators.

accounts of financial and nonfinancial concerns leads to an unwieldy fusing of data defying fruitful analysis. Furthermore, since public policy would prohibit the merging of a manufacturing company and a bank into a single corporation, treatment of a group containing such dissimilar units as though it were a single, completely integrated company is not feasible. In addition the crowning consideration seems to be that, under existing laws regulating the activities of financial institutions, a subsidiary bank is unlikely to devote any important part of its resources to financing affiliated enterprises of a nonfinancial type. Consequently the bank may be considered as external to the area of integrated operations. In consolidation the procedure called for, then, is to retain the investment account of the parent company, and to supplement the consolidated reports with the statements of the bank or other financial corporation as a legal unit.

Somewhat similar in type are the cases involving combinations of companies entirely within the nonfinancial sector of the economy. The reference here is to situations involving manufacturing corporations, mining companies and transport or manufacturing units, and similar combinations. Relationships of this nature are not in general frowned upon nor would there be, for example, widespread opposition on legal or other grounds to the fusion into one corporation of a manufacturing company and a series of already-controlled retail outlets.[18] But still the problem remains. In cases of complete or partial vertical integration through shareholdings, is consolidation of all controlled companies to take place or is it to be restricted to companies within a given industrial sector? Although apparently similar to the case of a bank controlled by a manufacturing company, these cases are not identical. Noninclusion may not be supported on the grounds that single-corporate units performing the same variety of functions do not exist; in these situations the simplifying device of treating the affiliated units "as though but one existed" may legitimately be employed. Again the important consideration appears to be whether or not the affiliated companies carry on extensive intercorporate operations. If they do, noninclusion cannot be argued, as with the bank, on the grounds of virtual exclusion from consolidated affairs.

[18] The following passage is found in the explanatory notes of Table II in the Securities and Exchange Commission's series, Survey of American listed corporations: "It should be noted that instructions . . . permit registrants to withhold the name of subsidiaries which . . . are 'retail subsidiaries' of a registrant which is not directly or through subsidiaries primarily engaged in merchandising at retail. . . ." Is this provision included to permit withholding of trade connections from competitors or from the public?

As an example, assume an automobile company controls a body plant, a glass factory, a steel company, a woodworking corporation, a sawmill, and an installment finance agency. Provided all the constituent units are closely linked in operations, and provided they deal almost exclusively with each other and only incidentally with other enterprises, an integrated area of operations exists and, despite the dissimilarity of functions performed, consolidation appears to be in order. However, if the installment finance agency, for example, has been acquired primarily as an investment, and does a general financing business only a fraction of which is with the customers of the parent or its affiliates, exclusion of that unit from consolidation is proper. A similar conclusion holds for any other constituent unit not an integral part of the combination as an operating entity.

In essence the notion of centralized control as it applies to consolidated statements has been clarified by including the condition that unitary operations also exist. In a fundamental sense this clarification is essential. It permits a distinction to be maintained between centralized control as an expression of individual or group influence and as a device for welding together a functioning business unit. In the language of logic, centralized control is a necessary condition for consolidation but not sufficient. In addition to control truly integrated or related operations must be present.

According to Dewing the group in control of the Du Pont company, directly and indirectly, also dominates both General Motors Corporation and United States Rubber Company. But despite the unified control the three companies are not ordinarily considered as constituting a combination calling for the preparation of consolidated reports because the business operations of each company are distinct from those of the others. "A unity of control exists in form but not in substance. And, in consequence, or rather in spite of the condition, each of these corporations is an individual business possessing a unity and an individuality of its own." [19] In a similar manner Dewing refers to the Stone and Webster organization which has immediate control through management contracts over a number of electric utilities. No evidence exists, however, that these utilities are operated as parts of a single company; therefore consolidation of accounts is not called for.

---

[19] A. S. Dewing, Financial policy of corporations. Fourth edition. (New York, 1941):898, note (d).

Investments in nonintegrated controlled companies then assume a status in consolidation analogous to that accorded nonoperating assets in a single-company balance sheet. If investments of this type are numerous or quantitatively significant, a group statement may be submitted as an exhibit amplifying the asset shown in the consolidated balance sheet. In addition the heading of the consolidated statements should indicate as concisely and completely as possible the types of companies included in consolidation, together with an explanatory note revealing the controlled companies excluded and the reasons for noninclusion.

National Concentration as a Standard

Of the subsidiaries of corporations registered with the Securities and Exchange Commission on June 30, 1938, over 20 per cent were incorporated abroad.[20] If there is increased American participation in international affairs after the war foreign investments are likely to receive a sharp stimulus. In view of the evident policy of the Federal government to outlaw the cartel affiliations of United States corporations, the financial mechanism adopted will probably consist in large part of the creation of foreign branches and subsidiaries. As a consequence the problem of the treatment in consolidation of companies in other lands will continue to be of importance. Of course no one is in a position to foresee the conditions under which international investments will be carried on. On the basis of the experience of the past two decades, however, certain characteristic difficulties may be discussed.

An important problem arises from the almost inevitable existence of diverse corporation laws in different countries. For example, concerning its English subsidiary F. W. Woolworth Company reports that "although it owns 52.7 per cent of the ordinary shares of the British Company, it does not have the power under British law to initiate the declaration of dividends." [21] Restrictions of this nature at best limit the extent to which effective control may be exercised; under more stringent regulations effective control might well be impossible. To the extent, however, that foreign shareholders collaborate with the controlling interest these provisions are merely irritants and do not destroy the conditions of consolidation. It is hardly likely that a corporation would acquire or establish a foreign subsidiary in the face of

[20] Securities and exchange commission. Statistics of American listed corporations. Part I, page 29.

[21] Accountants' handbook. Third edition: 1098.

local prohibitions effectively preventing control, but the restrictions might very well be enacted subsequently. As a result a continuing examination of foreign business regulations is essential in order to determine whether or not a constituent unit has been converted into a mere foreign investment. As soon as the obstructions become onerous enough to render integrated operations impossible the subsidiary should be dropped from consolidation and the investment therein classified as non-operating.

In addition to specific restraints on control of local companies, a foreign country may place general obstacles in the way of the free transfer of funds, culminating in some instances in outright prohibition of the export of foreign exchange. So long as the restrictions remain on the financial level merely to force transfers through officially designated channels or to implement some phase of monetary policy, essential unity of operations is not destroyed. The hazards of foreign operations are probably thereby increased but their nature is not materially changed. In a sense restrictions of this type are a commonplace everywhere, except that usually they are imposed by contract, not by governmental decree. For example, a domestic subsidiary may be restrained by a bond indenture from paying dividends or lending money until provision is made for creditors. A curtailment of this kind in domestic affairs is usually not considered severe enough to warrant excluding the subsidiary from consolidation, and complications in foreign affairs may be dealt with in a similar manner.

Where foreign exchange exports are prohibited entirely the traditional basis of international business operations is shorn away. In most instances the basis of continued unified operations is likewise seriously impaired. Assuming no commodity export-import prohibitions other than customary tariff barriers, however, a foreign subsidiary engaged in an extractive industry, processing basic raw materials, or manufacturing may easily continue to operate as an integral part of a far-flung international holding company empire. In such a case, the American parent would finance foreign operations and be reimbursed by bringing out of the foreign country the ores, metals, or manufactured products to be used or sold elsewhere. In a similar manner revenues from foreign sales could be recovered by purchasing raw or finished materials abroad and using them in other phases of a combination's operations. The impact of restrictions on funds transfers must therefore be determined in the light of operations actually carried on and the adjustments available to meet restraints.

Restrictions on transfers of commodities are by no means unknown. Again, as with foreign exchange prohibitions, the impact is usually specific, not general. Continued operations under these restrictions is usually a sufficiently valid indication that integrated activity has not been destroyed. The imposition of new, unforeseen hindrances, however, may cause a fundamental reorganization of a concern. Pending definite evidence of its ability to adapt itself to the changed environment, exclusion from consolidation seems the proper policy to follow.

Thus far the discussion has been preoccupied with the problem of the existence of a consolidated group. Granting the existence of a combination, the related question is then posed of the procedure to be followed in the presence of unstable exchange rates. In consolidating the accounts of a parent and its foreign subsidiary the resultant must be expressed in terms of a common denominator, presumably the local currency in which the accounts of the parent are kept. As long as exchange rates are highly stable, fluctuating within narrow, well-defined limits such as the former gold points, the task of translating a foreign currency into local terms is purely mechanical and presents no serious theoretical problems. The gains or losses resulting from slight fluctuations in rates may then be easily absorbed as inevitable accompaniments of a business conducted in this manner. When rates fluctuate violently over short periods of time, however, the resulting discrepancies may not be ignored. They represent speculative gains or losses and, as such, distinction should at least be made between those already realized and those resulting from the accidental effect of the rate of exchange prevailing on the balance-sheet date.

For example, the conventional rule in foreign exchange accounting with respect to current assets is to convert them at the rate prevailing on the date of the statement. Assume that a foreign subsidiary purchases merchandise at cost from its domestic parent at a time when the exchange rate is 10 to $1; assume further that some of the merchandise is unsold at the end of the accounting period, that inventories are to be shown at cost in consolidation, and that the exchange rate is now 20 to $1. If the rule cited is followed, the subsidiary's inventory will be converted to a dollar value of one-half its cost; the consolidated inventory figure is not at cost, but at cost less a speculative loss occasioned by an unfavorable turn in the foreign exchange market.

The rule usually adopted for depreciation of fixed assets calls for conversion of depreciation provisions at the rates at which the fixed asset has been included in the balance sheet. But notice the effect of this procedure on consolidated reporting:

> These charges may be materially greater or less than the present dollar equivalent of the annual charges for depreciation entered in currency in the subsidiary company's accounts (which would presumably be calculated on the basis of the currency cost). Should the effect be that taking all the foreign subsidiaries together the aggregate dollar depreciation charge on a branch accounts basis is materially less than the present dollar equivalent of the aggregate currency charges contained in the subsidiaries' accounts, the effect may be to increase the consolidated profits to an amount greater than would be received were the subsidiaries to pay in dividend and remit in dollars the whole of the foreign currency profits shown by their accounts. If this should occur it might be necessary to transfer the excess to a special reserve or otherwise deal with it so as to preclude it from treatment as a profit of the holding company; in cases of serious distortion due to this cause the propriety of consolidating the accounts at all might require consideration.[22]

The dilemma is real, and the resulting distortion may be serious. To avoid a misrepresentation of consolidated assets the subsidiary's records must be ignored and accrued depreciation computed as though the asset were purchased and used in this country; if this is done, however, the comparability of the computed dollar profits with the converted profit computation of the subsidiary is destroyed. To a limited extent hedging operations are possible to absorb the risk on short-term operations such as receivables and payables, but no similar mechanism is available to minimize the effects of a dual monetary standard on fixed assets and depreciation.

Inability to reconcile the conflicting demands of two currencies subject to erratic and uncorrelated fluctuations may necessitate the abandonment of consolidation of accounts. This step should be taken, however, only as a last resort after all possibilities of reconciliation through explanatory notes and other devices have been exhausted. Where nonconsolidation is decided upon, a group statement of the excluded subsidiaries may be feasible and represent the best available substitute for complete consolidation.[23] Since a group statement merely purports to exhibit a

---

22 T. B. Robson, "The construction of consolidated accounts," *The accountant* (London), XCIV:364–81 (March 7, 1936). Where the original says "sterling" I have substituted "dollar" or "dollars."

23 A group statement as contrasted with a consolidated statement may be defined as a combined statement from which the controlling interest is absent.

segment of combined operations the formal requirements for its preparation are less rigid than those for a consolidated balance sheet. For example, all South American subsidiaries might be presented in one group statement and European subsidiaries in another; alternatively, the line of cleavage might run between foreign manufacturing and sales subsidiaries. Furthermore, in the face of irreconcilable exchange fluctuations no serious objections may be made to the practice of presenting the group statement in terms of the foreign currency, together with a brief résumé of pertinent exchange gyrations.

Group statements are also available to support the investment account for controlled companies excluded from consolidation for reasons other than foreign exchange instability. In general, however, the device of a group statement should be employed cautiously under these circumstances because of the temptation to exclude companies from consolidation rather freely and to submit a group statement instead. Only when inclusion of controlled subsidiaries is clearly unsatisfactory or impossible should the group statement be introduced.

By way of contrast, the use of group statements should be encouraged for companies included in consolidation. A consolidated statement of a vertically integrated combination, for example, is made more useful if group statements are appended, one each for all manufacturing subsidiaries, all transport companies, all mining enterprises, and the like. The group statement in this usage is not a substitute for consolidation but an amplification; consequently no fear need be felt that its employment will replace desired consolidation of accounts.

Consistency of Treatment as a Standard

In delineating the proper area over which consolidation may occur, procedures must be adopted which will result in comparability of statements from period to period. Changes will occur, of course, in any going concern, and the reflection of these changes is an essential part of all accounting. Distinction must be maintained, however, between alterations resulting from business activities and those imposed in response to a new conception of the problem at hand.

For example, subsidiaries over which control has been newly acquired must be included in consolidation; no inconsistency results from the presence of more constituent units this period than last. If the concern has expanded, that fact must be reported and the results incorporated in the statements. An inconsistency does occur, however, if last period temporarily controlled companies were included, and this period such companies are excluded. In this latter case the consolidated area has been redefined, a procedure to be avoided unless imperatively demanded by the fact that former procedures are now known to be wholly indefensible and therefore are properly to be abandoned. Whenever it is necessary to make a purely technical shift of this type in the area of consolidation, specific attention should be called to it and an estimate made of the effect of the change on important categories, such as profits, surplus, current assets, etc. In this way deliberate or unintentional misstatement of a concern's progress will be avoided. The consistency under discussion, in other words, is of the type congenial to the underlying concept of an integrated area of operations.

The proper treatment of investment in companies controlled incidentally or temporarily has already been indicated. Adherence to the going-concern concept requires their exclusion from consolidation since they are not an integral part of a concern's operations. They will, of course, be included as investments along with other similar holdings in nonaffiliated companies.

For the same reason, companies in process of promotion, liquidation, or reorganization should be excluded. So long as they continue in the status indicated they are not functioning as parts of a going concern. With respect to promotion and liquidation, this treatment seems eminently proper. As to reorganization, however, caution must be exercised to avoid excluding cases in which the reorganization is purely formal, not interfering with the normal activities of the business. The reference is limited, then, to those cases in which the ordinary functions of a company are at least temporarily suspended.

The treatment accorded companies whose status has changed must turn on the nature of the altered circumstances. A new unit, for example, formerly in the promotional stage but now in full operation, is to be included as a full-fledged member of the combination. Similarly a reorganized company is restored once more to its place as a constituent unit of the consolidation. A change, however, from a position as a subholding company to that of a company without subsidiaries calls for no shift in treatment, provided the same functions as formerly are still performed by the group involved. In like manner any rearrangement of companies for purely administrative reasons or in response to regulatory prescription does not warrant a redefinition of the limits of the concern unless new units are added or old ones dropped. The test to be applied is on the basis of operations conducted—does the reorganized group continue to perform the same functions as before? If so, essentially the same combination exists; if not, the area of integrated operations has changed and so must the area of consolidation.

According to a report of the Securities and Exchange Commission, about one-fourth of all registered corporations use a fiscal year other than the calendar year.[24] It is probable, then, that in some instances, at least, constituent units employ dissimilar fiscal years. This situation is particularly likely to occur and in some measure to be encouraged by accountants if affiliated companies are widely separated geographically. Where such is the case the statements and reports of each company must be made up sufficiently in advance to permit the preparation of holding company and consolidated statements shortly after the close of the dominant company's fiscal year. As a consequence, while the practice may be condemned on general grounds, its existence and probable continuation must be recognized.

Clearly a company may not be excluded from consolidation merely because its accounting period terminates on a date different from the closing date of one or more affiliates. To permit exclusion on this basis would make the area of consolidation a function of an essentially arbitrary and perhaps shifting determination of the boundaries of the business year. By a mere reshuffling of closing dates, in other words, an individual or group in control could artificially alter the accounting projection of a concern's activities—an obviously undesirable situation.

Inclusion of companies with dissimilar fiscal years must be handled carefully and provision made for eliminating or at least reducing the effect of the overlapping of dates. The effect of transactions occurring between the close of a subsidiary's fiscal period and the date of a consolidated statement should be indicated, and handled on a consistent basis from year to year.[25]

One useful rule of general accounting procedure permits the waiving of all other rules when an item is so small that the manner of its treatment cannot possibly affect the validity of the statements. In consolidation, by simple extension, the same practice is found where companies are "not of material significance in relation to the total enterprise." This procedure, in essence a relaxing of all rules, may not, however, be used to produce dis-

---

[24] Securities and Exchange Commission. Statistics of American listed corporations. Part I, p. 31.

[25] See, e.g., the requirements of the Securities and Exchange Commission in Regulation S-X, and summarized briefly in Accountants' handbook. Third edition: 1065.

torted results. The lack of materiality referred to must be present both in an absolute and a relative sense. The noninclusion of one small company may be justified; the omission of thirty of them, together representing a significant segment of consolidated activity, may not be condoned on the ground that, taken one at a time, each is admittedly negligible in importance.

Summary

On the whole the present inquiry into the standards commonly employed to define the area of consolidation has resulted in the commonplace finding that accountants must exercise judgment. It was found impossible, for example, to formulate a workable standard merely on the basis of the size of a parent company's holdings of subsidiaries' shares. Even less objective is the use of "controlling influence" as a guide. Similarity of operations, geographical concentration, and consistency of treatment proved useful as partial standards but with too many exceptions and qualifications to warrant isolating them for exclusive attention.

The quest, however, has not been fruitless. Although the exercise of judgment is still essential, the judgment to be made concerns one central inquiry: does an area of integrated operations exist, and if so, where may a definite boundary line be drawn so that all constituent units are included and those not a part of the enterprise excluded? As a result of focussing attention on this leading query the judgment is removed from the realm of pure opinion, dependent for its validity on the integrity, knowledge, and good sense of the individual expressing it, to that of a process of examination and assessment of a limited variety of pertinent data—a process verifiable by others who may perform the same task. The criteria discussed, and others of similar type, then fall into place as allies in an attack on the problem. Together they point the way and forestall erroneous conclusions; they are continual reminders of the series of conditions necessary for integrated operations and emphasize the set of circumstances all of which must be present in order to sustain a judgment that consolidation is in order.

IV

ELIMINATION OF INTERCOMPANY TRANSACTIONS

ONCE THE AREA of consolidation has been satisfactorily delineated consolidation of accounts, in the narrow technical sense, may properly proceed. The techniques adopted to weld together the accounts of legally separate units must be designed to produce the intended accounting projection of a unified enterprise. In the search for appropriate tools it is natural to explore the kit employed in single-company accounting.

A characteristic feature of consolidation is the elimination of intercompany transactions. Immediately a close analogy is suggested between home office-branch accounting and the similar problems involved in a parent-subsidiary relationship—an analogy that seems particularly appropriate in view of insistence on restricting consolidation to the area of integrated operations. The same reasons operate in both situations to sustain elimination of intercompany transactions and accounts. In both instances evidences of interdepartmental relationships are ignored as irrelevant; in both, the accounts are retained which reflect the assets of the accounting entity involved, and its debts to legal persons outside the entity.

The branch accounting analogy has its limitations; consequently it may not be pushed too far in framing a solution to the consolidation problem. For example, a minority interest is unknown to branch accounting; therefore, a guide to the proper treatment of outside interests in consolidation must be sought elsewhere. Within the limits of the analogy, however, branch accounting supplies a familiar, easily accessible technique for treating many intercompany relationships. Likewise, within the limits of the analogy are found most of the consolidating techniques on which there seems to be virtually unanimous agreement.

The practice of eliminating intercompany receivables and payables is wholly consistent with the basic premise of an economic or business entity. No criticism of the practice of recording intercompany short-term debts in the books of the affiliated corporations follows from their elimination in consolidation. Detailed intercompany accounts are still essential parts of a complete accounting, but they have no effect on the status of the whole enterprise viewed as a unit. They arise as the result of transfers of assets from one affiliate to another, from the performance of intercompany services, or from the creation of intercompany obligations through dividend declarations or otherwise. The payment of these debts shifts cash from one constituent unit to another with no consequent direct effect on the total cash resources of an affiliated group. By the same token, nonpayment has no effect on the total cash of the group and, as a result, no significance may be attached in the consolidated statements to any entries or accounts reflecting actual or estimated intercompany bad debts.

Long-term loans between affiliates are likewise eliminated in consolidation. Borrowings against bonds or notes by one constituent unit from a related company transfers cash but does not move it outside the area of unified operations. An inflation of the totals assigned to assets and debts is avoided by removing from each the amount of purely intercompany conveyances. In like manner the accrual and payment of interest on these loans are submerged as not affecting an enterprise's status or operations. Interest income reflected on the lender's books is offset against the reciprocal interest deduction recorded by the borrower.

The principle of elimination is general and applies to intercompany shareholdings and dividends as well as to the conventional indicators of a debtor-creditor relationship already described. A parent company's investment in subsidiaries' shares must be reconciled with the latter's proprietary accounts and then cancelled against them. Certain characteristic problems of consolidation, and disagreements over their solution, arise from this process of reconciliation and cancellation and are therefore discussed in detail below. On the general principle of elimination, however, there is no disagreement: accounts evidencing purely intercorporate relationships are to be submerged. Since intercompany shareholdings are omitted, the same treatment is accorded dividends on those investments.

In accordance with this general principle, intercompany sales and purchases are usually omitted from total consolidated merchandising activities. Because the whole transaction is treated as though it had never occurred, no attention need be paid to the prices at which the exchanges took place. With respect to intercompany transfers of assets still remaining in the area of consolidation, however, attention must be paid to the recorded prices since characteristically they may still show markups or markdowns on purely interdepartmental movements. Concerning the treatment of these deviations, some disagreement exists. This type of situation will therefore be examined more carefully in a subsequent section.

Although no instance is at hand of dissent with the objective of offsetting intercompany purchases and sales, some criticism is occasionally voiced to carrying merely the net figure into a consolidated statement. For example, assuming total sales of $1,000,000, of which $400,000 were intercompany, it is contended that both the gross figure and the deduction should be shown explicitly rather than merely the difference of $600,000. This contention is based on the consideration that analysis of statements is easier if both figures are shown. Specifically a comparison of sales with consolidated capital is envisaged in order to determine rates of turnover. Obviously the rates are lower if the net figure is employed than if the total sales volume is used. Consequently the turnover rates for the consolidation will probably be lower than the corresponding rates for any important constituent unit. There is nothing, however, either improper or strange in this result. Other things being equal, when the size of a business unit is increased from a single corporation to an affiliated group an increase occurs in the period of process—the average length of time it takes for a unit of commodities to pass through the combination. A similar result is observable when a single corporation expands, particularly in the direction of vertical integration. The proper comparison, then, is between the turnover rates of a combination and those of other enterprises of comparable size performing similar functions, not between those of a combination and a single company engaged in merely one step in the productive process. It must be admitted, however, that for purposes of consolidation no essential requirement is violated if both a gross figure and a deduction for intercompany transfers are shown. In this and other similar instances, therefore, deference may be made to the wishes of those who find it difficult to make the transition from consideration of the characteristics of legally separate units to those of combined operations.

The practice of intercompany eliminations is also applied to all other instances of offsetting revenue-expense accounts. Royalties on patents owned by an affiliate, rents on properties of an associated company, and management fees for services performed by a parent or other subsidiary are examples of charges appearing as expenses or production costs on one set of books and as revenues on another. Except for consideration of intercompany markups resulting from transactions of this type on assets still held within the consolidated area, the resultant charges and credits are offset.

Certain types of contingent liabilities also disappear from consolidated statements in accordance with the eliminations procedure. This occurs when the contingent liability is in reality a duplication of a debt to outsiders already reflected on the records. For example, a parent company may guarantee the principal and interest of a subsidiary's bond issue. The debt evidenced by the subsidiary's accounts with bonds and interest payable must be paid only once—under the assumed conditions, either by the subsidiary or by the parent as guarantor. From the point of view of the consolidation, since the effect on consolidated resources is identical in either eventuality, the precise disbursing unit is a matter of insignificant detail. As a consequence the contingency may be ignored and the matter disposed of after assurance that the debt is properly reflected in the subsidiary's accounts.

A similar analysis and treatment is pertinent in the event one company discounts an affiliate's note outside the area of consolidation. The company discounting the note is contingently liable as endorser, and may reflect this situation in a notes receivable discounted account. The company issuing the note is of course primarily liable and shows this fact in notes payable. In consolidation the notes receivable discounted account, expressing the contingency, is suppressed and only the primary liability on the note is included. Other contingency conditions must be examined in like fashion to determine if the principle of intercompany elimination applies.

Universal agreement on the necessity of offsetting intercompany items raises a pertinent query concerning the treatment of the related accounts on the statements of the constituent companies. If a subsidiary sells one-half its output to affiliates, should this information be revealed in the subsidiary's own reports? If this information is reflected should the amount of intercompany markup involved be indicated?[1] Since all intercompany transactions are eliminated in preparing consolidated statements, the questions posed are clearly not applicable to that problem. The mechanical difficulties of consolidation are undoubtedly reduced if this information is already available in the statements of constituent companies but no alteration in principle results from its presence or absence. Nevertheless, a complete accounting for all elements of the integrated group calls for some consideration of the problem raised.

Aside from management, which would probably already be in possession of the indicated information, the groups to whom the

[1] For example, Kohler, in another connection, states: "Outside stockholders are entitled to know what portion of their book equities is represented by a 'controlled' profit; that is, a profit that has not yet been realized through a sale to the public." *Accounting review*, XIII:68.

data might be of value are the outside shareholders and the creditors of the subsidiary. These groups certainly should recognize that intercompany transactions are carried on between associated parties, and may not be on a strict commercial basis; they may, however, properly expect and insist that, as long as a dominant company refuses or is not required to assume legal responsibility for a subsidiary's debts or to recognize outside shareholders as part of the controlling group, the prices dictated by a dominant company be high enough to protect their interests. The extent to which the legal profits of a subsidiary are "controlled" is of no consequence; of prime importance is the extent to which its profits are being reduced or liquid assets drained off by a discriminatory price policy administered by a dominant company. Some light may be thrown on this phase of the situation by a separation in subsidiaries' statements of transactions with outsiders and transactions with affiliates. Insistence by accountants on this procedure will provide a subsidiary's creditors and outside shareholders with the data on which to decide whether or not to withdraw from the company or, in rare instances, to take steps to force a change in a dominant company's tactics.

Another cognate issue is raised by an amendment to Regulation S-X of the Securities and Exchange Commission.[2] With respect to investments in securities of affiliates and indebtedness of affiliates, a company must indicate in its balance sheet the amounts eliminated and those not eliminated in consolidation. The reasonableness of this requirement seems evident, and is not the problem at issue here. What is of importance is the question of elevating this specific ruling into a general principle to be followed in all phases of the preparation of constituent companies' statements. Consistent classification of all items into the amounts cancelled and not cancelled in consolidation produces two important related consequences. First, by indicating the explicit links between the two, closer integration is provided between a consolidated report and the statements from which it is constructed. Emphasis is thereby forcibly directed to the nature of a consolidated report as a combination of single statements. Second, the consolidated statement is accorded a preëminent position. Constituent statements containing direct reference to corresponding consolidated items assume in consequence the appearance of supporting schedules. Their form and content, in other words, are dictated in large part by the requirements of the master report—the consolidated statement.

---

[2] Accounting series release No. 24 (May 23, 1941): 2. Regulation S-X, Rule 5–02, as amended.

Of similar import is the technical device of a consolidating statement—in reality, a highly condensed worksheet containing the data of each constituent company, the major eliminations, and the resultant combined picture. It is superior to the practice of labeling items in each constituent report in that all essential data are presented as parts of a single, unified schedule rather than in the form of scattered references in possibly a multitude of balance sheets and income statements. As a useful device for incorporation in published statements, however, the consolidating statement is sharply limited because its proper interpretation requires knowledge of the technical features of consolidation.

The whole approach of this monograph is clearly favorable to developments of the type just mentioned. Any procedure emphasizing the unified nature of a combination through stock ownership and the relationships existing among its constituent parts is to be welcomed and fostered. The more attention we are forced to pay to an explicit showing of the interrelationships and operations of this type of combination the more careful we will be to make certain integrated operations do exist. When they do exist and the proper boundaries are drawn consolidated reports become immediately the obvious vehicle for an accounting expression of the situation. Abuses in the form of careless consolidation and slipshod combination of accounts will then probably become rarer and the partial disrepute into which consolidated statements have fallen will become less marked.

The controversies which exist concerning the proper consolidating procedure center around a few rather well-defined, characteristic situations, namely, (a) the treatment of investments in affiliated companies, (b) the reconciliation of identical items appearing on two sets of books at different values, (c) the effect of the presence of outside interests, and (d) the nature of consolidated surplus. The discussion of these points of friction will occupy most of the remainder of this monograph. An attempt will be made to resolve these problems by an appeal to the basic premises previously discussed.

V

INTERCOMPANY INVESTMENTS AND OTHER ASSETS

Investments in Affiliates on Owner's Books *

TWO METHODS of recording investments in affiliated companies are prominently advocated, and a third method is sometimes proposed. The first procedure calls for initial entry of the shares at cost or other acquisition value, with no subsequent adjustments except for purchases and sales, partial liquidation of

---

* EDITORIAL NOTE.—Dr. Moonitz characterizes this section as an "extended digression," and points out that "satisfactory consolidated statements may be prepared regardless of a parent's method of recording its investments." In view of these admissions it is somewhat hard to see why he considered it necessary to include this material in his study. Moreover, in my opinion his objections to the cost basis of recording investments, and the related arguments for the "book value method," are not decisive. He is recommending, in effect, that the parent company keep its own accounts from the consolidated point of view, and were his recommendation adopted there would be little excuse left for preparing consolidated statements. That is, the main reason for the preparation of such statements is to show the stockholders of the parent or dominant company what the amount of the controlling equity is, assuming corporate lines to be erased, and if this is done in terms of the regular accounts of the holding company there is not much point to going further. Early in his study the author concludes that "consolidated statements must be regarded as auxiliary, special-purpose reports, not primary, all-purpose exhibits supplanting or displacing the statements of legally recognized entities." In his effort to demolish the cost basis of accounting for investments he seems to forget that his proposal is not entirely consistent with the earlier basic conclusion.

The time may come when the corporate institution recognized by the law as a separate entity, will lose part or all of its force as a distinct accounting entity, but we are not yet at that point. Under present conditions the corporation is not merely the steward or agent of the stockholder, and the income of the corporation is not realized, recognizable income to the stockholder. And this is just as true in the case of a large, dominant stockholder as in that of the minority investor. Even the stockholder holding 100% of all shares is not in the same position as the sole proprietor of an unincorporated activity.

In another connection Dr. Moonitz criticizes "compromise" points of view. But here he undertakes to make a case for a method of procedure which represents compromising with a vengeance. He adopts the phrase "book value method," but this is a misnomer. The procedure he is recommending calls for the use of actual cost to the stockholder as a basis of accounting for the investment to cover the entire subsidiary equity at date of acquisition, regardless of the amount appearing in the subsidiary's accounts at that date, and recognizes subsidiary book value only with respect to changes therein after the date of acquisition. This amounts to completely rejecting subsidiary income accounting prior to acquisition and completely accepting such accounting thereafter. I see no real defense for such a hodgepodge procedure, except, perhaps, to "facilitate the mechanics of consolidation" (a defense rejected by the author).

capital, or fundamental alterations in the nature of the investment, such as a reorganization of the subsidiary. The second procedure likewise enters the shares initially at acquisition price but adjusts the investments account for the parent's equity in all subsequent variations in subsidiaries' capital. The third procedure involves initial entry at book value, regardless of acquisition price, with continuous revision to reflect book value at all times.

It should be kept in mind that satisfactory consolidated statements may be prepared regardless of a parent's method of recording its investments. Given the method employed, a technical reconciliation and elimination may be readily devised to accord with the parent's accounting practices and the requirements of consolidation. Consequently, the acceptance of the recommendations made in this monograph to make consolidated statements consistent with the entity principle does not require adherence by a parent company to any particular method of accounting for investments. Viewed in this light, the present section is in the nature of an extended digression—a digression covering a topic which acquires significance because of the characteristically large proportion of a holding company's total assets represented by investments, and because of the special qualitative nature of these investments as reflections of an interest in *controlled* subsidiaries.

The first procedure, maintaining the investment account at cost, is strongly advocated as consistent with the rules prevalent

---

The author concludes that "in every concrete situation, with the exception of common stock dividends on common shares and of preferred dividends in arrears, book value functions more smoothly than the cost rule." I am not convinced that this conclusion is justified, assuming that it refers to the process of holding company accounting rather than to the mechanics of consolidation. Bearing in mind the importance of cost data and realized income figures for tax purposes, and in other connections, the lack (in many cases) of detailed control of or intimate information regarding the income accounting of the affiliate, the absence (in many cases) of complete consistency in the accounting of holding company and subsidiary, the difficulty of apportioning the rights in subsidiary earned surplus between two or more classes of stock, the importance of dividend action from a legal point of view and the fact that (in many cases) such action is not and should not be based merely on the condition of the holding company or the views of the immediate management of such company, it seems very clear to me that the cost basis of accounting for investments in other corporations, coupled with a recognition of income thereon as realized, is generally the simplest and most practicable basis available to the stockholder.

In "Some Tentative Propositions Underlying Consolidated Reports," published in the *Accounting Review*, March, 1938, E. L. Kohler made the following statement: "No practical benefits are derived from accruing profit and loss of subsidaries on the books of the controlling company; reserves for losses on investments in subsidiaries are preferably based on estimates of ultimate realization rather than on amounts of operating losses." With this statement I heartily concur.—W. A. PATON in recording the long-term investments of an unaffiliated corporation. It assumes that the cost rule is applicable to investments as well as other assets, in the process of matching revenues and outlays through the life of the enterprise. The emphasis is placed on a conventional accounting for the holding company alone, without regard to its position as the kingpin of the consolidated structure. This treatment is likewise consistent with the legal doctrine that each corporate unit is a separate compartment, insulated from other corporations, and oblivious of what goes on inside the barriers surrounding them. Until the other corporations act, through declaration of dividends or through formal reorganization, for example, any available evidence of changes in the status of one company's investment in another must accordingly be ignored completely.

In opposition to this method it should be pointed out that the cost rule is in large part a reaction to a world of uncertainty, and in that respect is inapplicable to relationships between a parent and a controlled affiliate. In the face of uncertainty, to cling to those things which are known is natural, and the cost rule then serves a useful purpose, but the rule should not be used to create an appearance of uncertainty where none exists. The affairs of a controlled company are generally as well known to a parent company as its own; consequently the practice of carrying the investments at cost can not be effectively defended on the basis of lack of adequate knowledge. Moreover, it may be noted that the cost rule has never been consistently applied to purely financial relationships, as evidenced by the treatment in general accounting of interest, discount, and premium on bonds and notes, of receivables and payables, and of cash. Its proper sphere is with respect to the nonfinancial items, inventories and fixed operating assets in particular, where the "pool of costs" concept is most appropriate. Aside from this general criticism the specific applicability of the cost rule to intercompany shareholdings is far from clear. The history of a dominant holding company is largely the history of its investments; to leave the record of those investments to the vagaries of a subsidiary's controlled dividend policy is to omit the crucial phase of that history and place the emphasis on relatively unimportant factors. So long as the law, for specific purposes, insists on treating a dominant company as a distinct entity, accounting must conform to the extent of distinguishing, for example, between profits available and those not available for dividends. But this is no new problem created by combination through stock ownership. In single-company records accountants have shown sufficient ingenuity in preserving a distinction between accounting profits, profits available for dividends, and taxable income to warrant the belief that they may do the same for a parent company, if they are so inclined.

The practice of initial entry at cost with adjustments of the investments accounts by a parent's proportion of its subsidiaries' subsequent gains or losses is compatible with a recognition of the special relationships existing among affiliated companies, and is the method advocated here. The integrated nature of the operations involved is recognized in correcting the investments accounts as soon as a change in an affiliate's status, measured presumably in accordance with conventional accounting procedures, is determined. Emphasis is thereby placed on the strategic consideration that the status of the investments varies with the fortunes of the units controlled, and not on the movements of cash. The effect of this method on a parent's income is to recognize it in the period when it actually arose and in its proper amount, not in the period or the amount in which cash flowed in response to a dividend declaration. On this aspect of the situation the Securities and Exchange Commission has made the following observations:

> If the determination of whether a holding company derives a material part of its income from its public utility subsidiaries were to rest solely on the basis of cash actually received, the parent company would then be in a position to assure itself of an exemption (from regulation) simply by preventing the distribution of earnings of its public utility subsidiaries. . . . For this reason, among others, we are of the opinion that all sources of income, including undistributed income of subsidiaries, must be taken into consideration.[1]

Within the limits set by contracts with creditors and others, a dominant company has full control over the financial aspects of the dividend policy of subsidiaries. Consequently a dominant company may initiate dividends according to policies of its own design, and, unless a strict cash basis of accounting is reverted to, lack of "realization" may not be urged as a decisive basis for nonrecognition of alterations in the investments accounts. Of equal importance, moreover, is the consideration that, in the absence of special circumstances, the validity of a subsidiary's profit computation is as well established as that of the parent itself. There is, therefore, no more reason for ignoring a subsidiary's records than for ignoring the similar computations of a parent's own operations.

[1] In the matter of Cities Service Co., 8 S.E.C., 326.

Initial entry at subsidiary book value with subsequent adjustments for the appropriate fraction of changes in the equities behind the investments is occasionally mentioned as an alternative to the method just discussed. For example, the Securities and Exchange Commission reports receipt of a proposal that "holding company investments be carried at amounts which reflect their equity in the subsidiaries on the basis of the underlying original cost of the subsidiaries' property, less appropriate depreciation and depletion reserves, and that any present excess over that amount be segregated and eventually eliminated." [2] In his criticism of the second method listed above, Paton states that "it would be more reasonable to adjust the investment account at date of acquisition to subsidiary book value, followed by periodic absorption of the holding company's share of subsidiary profits and losses. . . ." [3] This method has the undoubted merit of placing the investments accounts on all fours with the subsidiary's records, thus emphasizing in the most direct accounting manner possible what the investments stand for. The method in this form, however, is too uncritical; it forces the investment account of a parent into the mold set by a subsidiary's records as they stand at date of acquisition. When two conflicting measures of the same thing are present—the acquisition price of an investment in a subsidiary, on the one hand, and the subsidiary's proprietary accounts, on the other—it must not be assumed that one measure is always right and the other wrong or, stranger yet, that both may be correct at one and the same time. The disposition in consolidation of this discrepancy, the familiar problem of consolidated "goodwill," is discussed later on. At this point, however, it may be suggested that an intelligent attempt to correlate the investment accounts with book values would lead to a consideration of the adequacy of the subsidiary's underlying records. The discrepancy might turn out to be more apparent than real, provided a thorough-going appraisal of the subsidiary is made and the results incorporated in its records. In other words, the price paid by a parent for its investment might be nearer correct than the equity reflected on its subsidiary's books. Whether this proposition is valid clearly depends on the precise concrete situation involved; obviously no "solution" of the goodwill problem has

---

[2] Accounting series release no. 39 (December 19, 1942):2, referring to revisions in the Uniform System of Accounts for Public Utility Holding Companies. The proposal was rejected, but not without favorable comment.

[3] W. A. Paton, Advanced accounting (New York, 1941):763. In a continuation of the same passage Paton advocates the use of the strict cost basis, while admitting some logical force to the alternative of fair market value.

been derived. Nevertheless the difficulties associated with the reconciliation of investment accounts and the corresponding equities they represent would undoubtedly be minimized, Futhermore, an auditor of the parent's accounts would be more certain of the reasonableness of the values he was certifying.

A choice among the available methods obviously should not be made merely to facilitate the mechanics of consolidation. Under any method a satisfactory consolidations technique may be readily devised. The procedure chosen to record a parent's investments should be the one which accords most closely with the nature of the accounts involved. In the absence of a satisfactory explanation of a discrepancy between cost and book value, initial entry at cost seems appropriate because it results in a showing of the new application of resources but, at the same time, leaves a parent's total assets, debts, and capital unaffected. For the reasons already given, however, adherence to the "safe" practice of initial recording at cost is no barrier against using definite evidence of a changed value of a subsidiary's capital as a basis for adjusting the investments accounts.

The weakness of the strict cost method in reflecting the history of an investment in a controlled subsidiary is most apparent when it is applied to reorganizations of subsidiaries and to dividends declared by them.

Complete or quasi-reorganization of a subsidiary presents no conceptual difficulties to the book value method.[4] If the recorded equity back of the investments is changed, as under these circumstances it probably will be, the appropriate adjustments are made in the investment accounts in accordance with the routine already established for reflecting changes from any source in a subsidiary's capital. But the strict cost rule is incapable, without considerable strain, of absorbing such a shock. When a reorganization occurs this method must be abandoned, and a new "acquisition cost," dated from the time of reorganization, established.

A difficulty likewise confronts the cost rule in connection with dividends.[5] Under this rule these transfers of assets must be regarded as income to the parent, despite the fact that they reduce a subsidiary's earned surplus. The book value methods deal with the situation as it is—a receipt of assets by the parent in partial liquidation of its investments.

---

[4] In the balance of this section, "book value method" refers to the technique of initial entry in an investment account at cost, with adjustments for the parent's share of subsequent changes in its subsidiaries' proprietary equities.

[5] Unless otherwise indicated, the term "dividends" refers to cash and other property dividends, and excludes stock dividends.

Some recognition is given by the cost rule to this characteristic of all dividends in connection with those based on pre-acquisition surplus. For example, if a dividend is declared by a subsidiary immediately after the parent has acquired control, the parent's investment account is reduced by the amount of such dividend. In this situation the cost rule becomes, perforce, a book value method. All subsequent dividends must likewise be examined to see if any are based on preacquisition surplus; if so, the investment account must be reduced accordingly. The credits to income are therefore limited to dividends on subsidiaries' income generated after acquisition. In the event of reorganization the procedure under the cost rule is modified only to the extent of substituting generated "after reorganization."

The book value method requires no such distinction between preacquisition and postacquisition surplus. Since a dividend declaration reduces a subsidiary's proprietary equity, this method reflects the facts by crediting the parent's corresponding investment account and charging dividends receivable. This happens no matter when a dividend is declared and, therefore, the procedure need not consider the period in which the subsidiary's income arose. Income of the parent is recorded when income is recognized on the subsidiary's books. Profitable operations by a subsidiary result in an increase in its proprietary equity; therefore an increase in the parent's investment account is called for. Where the law treats this type of income as unrealized, the corresponding credit on a parent's books should be properly labelled to distinguish it from income legally available for a parent company's dividends.

The fundamental point at issue is the problem of the proper timing and amount of income accruing to a parent from its investments in affiliates. The contention here is that income accrues when the investments increase in value; the investments increase in value when the equities they represent grow; the equities of which they are a reflection grow when *bona fide* increases in subsidiaries' proprietary equities occur. In brief, income accrues to the parent at the same time that it accrues to the subsidiary and in an amount determined by the proportion of a subsidiary's capital owned by the parent. According to the cost rule recognizable income to the parent does not arise until dividends are declared and then only in an amount determined by the size of the dividend payment—this despite the fact that the dividend policy of a subsidiary is largely under the control of its parent. The cost rule, therefore, in this usage, is perilously close to becoming a form of the doctrine that income is identical with cash receipts.

Even under the assumptions that all subsidiaries declare dividends each period to the full extent of current earnings, and that no changes in subsidiaries' proprietary equities occur except as the result of operating losses and gains, the cost rule is unsatisfactory in that the decline in the value of investments in subsidiaries sustaining losses will not be reflected. If under the same assumptions the cost rule is modified to permit the adjustment of the investment accounts for losses, but not for gains, this difficulty would be eliminated and a correct showing of a parent company's income obtained. But notice that a proper result is obtained only under the special conditions postulated, and then only because dividend policy is geared to fit increases in capital while the investment accounts reflect changes in book value in the downward direction. In the usual cases, namely, when dividends are not identical in either magnitude or timing with current earnings and when some non-operating alterations in a subsidiary's proprietary equity are recorded, the cost rule, no matter how modified, fails to give results consistent with the known status of the investments. In general, because of the observed tendency of American corporations—subsidiaries as well as parents—to "plow back" part of the profits, the probabilities are that the cost rule will result in an understatement of a parent's income from investments in prosperous periods and an overstatement in time of depression, with understatement resulting over the cycle as a whole.

With respect to stock dividends of common stock on common, both the book value and cost methods require that no adjustment of investments accounts be made. This treatment is consistent with the nature of this type of stock dividend because no change in the equity behind common shares results from the transactions, and therefore no alteration occurs in the status of the shareholders. In other types of stock dividends, however, use of the cost rule requires recognition of the need for a special adjustment, whereas no modification of principle is required of the book value method.

For example, if the dividend takes the form of preferred shares on preferred, and is in lieu of the usual cash dividend on the preferred, the book value method immediately reflects the increased equity behind preferred shares by increasing the parent's investments in those stocks, with a corresponding credit to income. If the dividend is in addition to the regular cash dividend and the parent company also holds common stock, as will undoubtedly be the case, a corresponding decrease in its common stock investments will be recorded. The reduction of the equity of the common and the increase in that of the preferred shareholders is thus properly reflected on the parent's books. The cost rule is, however, in a quandary. If the procedure just described is followed, the cost rule becomes a book value method; if the dividend is ignored, expression is not given to a fundamental change in the history of the investments.

A dividend of preferred shares on common likewise presents no problem under a book value procedure. Assuming either no previously outstanding preferred shares or no arrearages on preferred already issued, the equity behind common shares is reduced by the amount of surplus capitalized and an equity of equivalent magnitude created for preferred. Therefore, the investments accounts are adjusted accordingly: increase the investment in preferred, decrease that in common. The cost rule presumably would record the transaction by a reassignment of the cost of the common shares held, and thus apparently preserve the tenets of entry at cost. Notice, however, that the magnitude of the new assignment of cost must be made on the basis either of relative book values or of relative market values of the two types of shares involved. In either event the independent variable is not cost. The cost rule itself contains no resources of its own capable of dealing with this kind of situation.

The remaining possibility—common shares on preferred—may be made the subject of a similar analysis. In the special case in which a parent owns identical percentages of common and preferred, no adjustment is called for under either method; if the parent already holds the same proportion of each class of shares, no change in that proportion results from the receipt of the dividend—the parent still owns the same percentage and amount as before of the equities behind each investment. The general case in which the proportionate holdings are dissimilar, however, brings about a new alignment of relative interests. According to the book value rule, the adjustment of the equity behind the common stock investment is calculated and recorded. If the percentage of preferred held is greater than that of common, the parent gains at the expense of the minority common stockholders; in the reverse case, the equity of the minority improves through a corresponding dilution of the parent's equity. As in the previous case of preferred on common holdings, the cost rule would presumably require a reassignment of cost. Again the cost rule is defective because it cannot encompass situations of this nature, save by the device of pleading an exception to the rule.

The existence of preferred dividends in arrears creates a problem not easily solved by any of the methods discussed. It is doubtful, because of the special nature of cumulative dividends, if any rule will give satisfactory results. In general, dividend arrearages confer no positive enforceable claims upon preferred shareholders; the benefits are contingent—those dividends must be liquidated before common stock may participate, but in the absence of a dividend declaration the claim is dormant. As the dividends accumulate, however, the equity behind the common shares diminishes. As a result the decline in the common stock investment accounts must presumably be reflected. In many cases, however, the arrearages are never removed completely by subsequent dividend declarations. Instead, as a device for meeting the cumulated dividend claims, the preferred shareholders are asked or compelled to accept some substitute for cash, perhaps more preferred shares, some common stock, or an issue of special notes or bonds. Consequently, until a compromise is actually effectuated no one is in a position to know precisely the impact of dividends in arrears on the equities of preferred and common, and, accordingly, it is difficult to frame entries to reflect the situation in a satisfactory manner. The probable result is that none of the methods would acknowledge a change until positive action was taken by the subsidiary's board of directors. In consolidation, however, an assignment of each company's surplus is made to the several classes of shares as though cumulative dividends in arrears were some day to be declared in full.

In every concrete situation, with the exception of common stock dividends on common shares and of preferred dividends in arrears, book value functions more smoothly than the cost rule. When applied to the investments of a parent company the cost rule is defective both on general theoretical grounds and in application to specific circumstances. The history of a parent's investments and its income from them may be correctly recorded only by reflecting in the parent's accounts the progress of the legal unit in which the investments are held.

Elimination of Intercompany Shareholdings

The existence of a discrepancy between cost and book value at date of acquisition makes difficult the direct elimination in consolidation of a parent's investment accounts and the corresponding proportion of its subsidiaries' proprietary equities. Before the difference may be properly disposed of the reasons for its existence must be determined, and the treatment followed should be in harmony with the conditions. Under no circumstances is it satisfactory to adopt a technical solution framed solely for the purpose of keeping the statements "in balance."

Acquisition of an investment in a subsidiary for a cash outlay not equal to the book value of the equity acquired may be the result of: (a) a gain or loss on the purchase, (b) errors in the accounting for specific assets or liabilities of the subsidiary, or changes in values of specific assets which have not been recorded; (c) an unassignable difference between book value and the market value of the subsidiary as a going concern. In a particular case, of course, more than one of these conditions may be present.

If the cash cost exceeds book value it is conceivable that the parent company sustained a loss on a purchase; conversely, acquisition at less than book value may indicate a profit. In view of the rather firmly established rule against recognizing gain or loss at time of purchase this possibility may be disposed of briefly. To sustain a finding of gain or loss, the position would have to be taken that the accounts of the subsidiary reflect its value properly and that the price reached by the parties was not in accord with such value. Such a position would be virtually impossible to sustain. While recognizing the theoretical possibility of its existence this explanation may, accordingly, be rejected as without concrete significance, at least in the great majority of cases.

By contrast with the gain-or-loss version of the discrepancy, an interpretation in terms of inappropriate valuation of a subsidiary's assets and debts seems more reasonable. Unsatisfactory depreciation policies, obsolescence of certain installations not acknowledged in the accounts, and inadequate treatment of deferred charges and credits are some of the reasons why book balances may be unreliable as a measure of fair market value. Moreover, even if no errors or inadequacies of the types just listed are assumed, it must be recognized that conventional accounting procedures are not geared to reflect exchange values. As a consequence it would be surprising indeed to find a case in which a company acquired an interest in a going concern at a fair price which exactly equated with book value.

Both an audit and an appraisal of a subsidiary are therefore desirable as the means of determining the extent to which the discrepancy may be accounted for by piecemeal revision of book figures. Of some help, perhaps, would be a parent's explanation of why it paid the price it did. On the whole, however, such evidence is unreliable, first, because many business men are unable to give an explicit accounting of the details entering into the setting of a purchase price and, second, because the explanation that is forthcoming is likely to contain large elements of self-justification and hindsight. Independent audit and appraisal are more apt to yield objective data capable of use in consolidation.

Introduction into the consolidated work sheets of the revised values derived for a subsidiary's assets and debts follows, then, as part of the process of reconciling investment accounts and the equities they represent. Whether or not the revised data may be fully incorporated into the subsidiary's records must be determined in accordance with the circumstances encountered in each case. On general grounds the revision of subsidiary book values is desirable. Since the subsidiary is now part of the area of integrated operations adjustment of its accounts to accord with the basis on which it was brought in would serve the useful purpose of welding it more firmly, on the accounting level at any rate, to its affiliates. However, there may be some objection to incorporating the results of appraisal as opposed to corrections based on audit. Finished goods, for example, may have been appraised on the basis of current market prices instead of the conventional cost basis, but it may still be desirable to maintain the inventory records of the subsidiary at cost. If the revised data are not introduced into the subsidiary's accounts, provision must be made for insuring their retention in appropriate manner in subsequent consolidated statements. Recognition in consolidation of an altered figure for equipment, for example, would require a corresponding correction of subsequent depreciation entries taken from the subsidiary's reports.

The discrepancy between cost and book value may not be completely explained by means of audit and appraisal. If the possibility of gain or loss on the purchase is excluded, the balance must be accounted for as an expression of intangible factors. When cost exceeds adjusted book value this intangible element may arise because the subsidiary possesses unrecorded goodwill or will acquire it as one result of affiliation.

The reasoning behind the assignment to goodwill of an otherwise unexplained excess of cost over book value is of importance and needs explicit recognition. In the absence of an acquisition gain or loss the conclusion is inescapable that the interest acquired was worth the price paid for it. The outlay in cash made by the parent is accepted as valid evidence of the value of the equity obtained. The excess may be due to tangible amounts capable of disclosure through the audit and appraisal of specific items or to intangibles attaching to the subsidiary as a going concern. In either event the values sustaining the purchase price are there; the problem reduces to one of measurement and recording. Confronted with a closed transaction presumably carried out in good faith and based on rational considerations this attitude toward the cash price is eminently reasonable. This interpretation carries with it the requirement that insofar as possible clear-cut expression be given to the values underlying the transaction. The measure available for this purpose is the price paid by the parent; the object to be measured is the proprietary equity of the subsidiary. The two are clearly related in magnitude; they are not, however, always identical in extent.

This reasoning holds for those who support recording the investment at book value as well as for the strict cost advocate. Cost as a basis for initial entry is justified when it provides objective evidence of the worth of a purchased item. To hold otherwise implies the acceptance of the bare fact of cash disbursement as sufficient to establish an equivalent asset in another form without regard to the object of the outlay, which might be to meet an adverse judgment in a damage suit, or the settlement of a tax deficiency. No one seriously advocates this alternative position. Any basis of measurement—cost, book value, market value, etc.—is valid only insofar as it is consistent with a rational interpretation of the transaction under scrutiny.

On the assumption then that a parent company's outlay is the best evidence available of the value of the interest acquired, the problem of measurement becomes one of applying this standard to the valuation of the subsidiary's capital. If a parent pays $150,000 for an entire proprietary equity recorded (after audit and appraisal) at $120,000, the conclusion follows that the fair value of that equity is $150,000. The difference of $30,000 is attributed to the omission on the subsidiary's records of goodwill. Consequently consolidated goodwill of $30,000 is introduced into the work sheets and the elimination of the related accounts is readily made.

If the parent paid $120,000 for an 80 per cent interest the same result should be obtained. A price of $120,000 for an 80 per cent interest indicates that the whole proprietary equity is worth $150,000; therefore consolidated goodwill is again $30,000. Similarly, if a 90 per cent interest is purchased for $135,000 the conclusion still follows that there is an unrecorded intangible factor of $30,000. The important point is that the price paid by the parent establishes a measure of the extent to which a subsidiary's total capital (in the broad sense) is understated because of the omission on its books of goodwill. In this connection the precise percentage of interest acquired by the parent is of secondary importance; the price paid is used to arrive at a fair valuation of the subsidiary.

The computation usually made yields results differing from those obtained above. Conventional procedure attributes a value to consolidated goodwill equal to the difference between the price paid and the book value of the portion of the equity acquired. For example, in the 80 per cent case above, the goodwill becomes $120,000 less $96,000, or $24,000; in the 90 per cent case, $135,000 less $108,000, or $27,000. The goodwill thereby becomes merely a gap-filler, an amount just sufficient to bring about a technical reconciliation of the offsetting accounts. The determination of the extent of understatement of a subsidiary's capital, however, should not depend on the size of a parent's investment. The parent paid the price it did because, presumably, the subsidiary is worth more than book value, and the amount of the excess does not vary with an alteration in the size of the parent's interest. The price paid is a measuring rod, a definite indicator of the relative magnitude of the understatement of the subsidiary's value; it does not create the value which already exists. The prior existence of value is the necessary condition sustaining the outlay as a rational act. Given the same set of facts with respect to parent and subsidiary—their competitive position, their accounting practices, the size of the new affiliated group, the methods by which the parent measured the value of the subsidiary, and the price per share paid by the parent—it is absurd to assign differing amounts to the subsidiary's goodwill solely on the basis of a variation in the number of shares acquired by the parent.

If consolidated goodwill is interpreted as a mere plug or balancing figure the amount may even be made to depend upon the method of costing investments employed by the parent. In a recent book on consolidated statements, "goodwill from consolidation" assumes four different values in response to the use of four methods of costing, namely, first-in, first-out, last-in, first-out, average cost, and specific identification. This startling result is obtained with identical proportionate holdings and identical prices assumed in each instance. [6]

The conventional procedure has been defended by reference to the rule that the recognition of goodwill is to be limited to the price paid for it. But the rule is clearly inapplicable to this situation. The parent company did not buy goodwill; it bought an interest in a subsidiary large enough to enable it to control the whole company, goodwill and all. When a parent holds a 90 per

6 E. J. B. Lewis, Consolidated statements (New York, 1942):61-3.

cent interest in a subsidiary, no one contends that it has bought 90 per cent of the cash, the receivables, the inventories, etc. In consolidation, conventional procedure is sound in requiring the inclusion of all the assets and debts of all the affiliates, except in the case of goodwill.

In general the explanations offered for the conventional solution appear to be mere rationalizations of a practice already deeply embedded in accounting routine. To judge from published statements the treatment of goodwill in practice is more direct and in some respects logically more satisfactory. Relatively few published consolidated statements show any goodwill at all, or, if they do, the amount assigned is purely nominal. It is highly improbable that the problem of reconciliation of cost and book value is absent from most actual situations; what is more likely is that the discrepancy is written off against consolidated surplus.[7] If this is the case the practice is consistent with the antipathy often expressed toward showing any goodwill at all. In other words, the attempt to revalue the subsidiary on the basis of acquisition price is abandoned; the excess over book value is viewed as of dubious significance, not possessing sufficient validity to warrant its inclusion in whole or in part in a consolidated statement. The existence or absence of goodwill is indicated, then, by the subsequent operating histories of each company and of the group as a whole. In one sense this treatment implies that the parent sustained a loss on the purchase of its interest in a subsidiary equal to the excess paid over book value. To this extent the practice is inconsistent with the usual injunction against recognizing acquisition gains or losses. This procedure is, nevertheless, superior to the treatment of the excess as a plug with which to fill a "hole" in the accounts. Either goodwill should be omitted altogether or, insofar as the available data permit, it should be shown in its entirety. To include only a fragment is defensible on neither logical nor practical grounds.

A similar discussion is applicable to the case in which the cash outlay is less than book value, and therefore need not be repeated in detail. The concept of "negative goodwill" or "allowance for general overvaluation" is of the same cloth as that of positive goodwill. The price paid indicates a going concern value of the subsidiary less than that shown on its books; accordingly, in the absence of a satisfactory explanation in terms of specific asset and liability items a blanket adjustment to write down the value of the subsidiary is required.

---

[7] See, for example, the annual report of Colgate-Palmolive-Peet Co. for the year ended December 31, 1940.

Occasionally the practice is encountered of absorbing the excess of book value over cost in consolidated surplus. This practice is tantamount to recognizing a profit on a purchase and therefore denies the position usually taken when cost exceeds book value that the interest acquired is worth what the parent paid for it. A logically consistent technique for disposing of the discrepancy may be developed by assuming either that the price paid by the parent or the book value of the subsidiary is the proper measure of the interest acquired, but cost may not be used in the one case and book value in the other.

With one important addition the same analysis as for the case of an investment acquired for cash may be applied to the use of a parent's capital stock as consideration. The discrepancy between par or stated value on the one hand and the book value of the interest acquired on the other may be in whole or in part a discount or premium on the parent's shares. If this is the situation the discount or premium should appear on the parent's books and be transferred from that source to the consolidated balance sheet. The difficulty lies, however, not in framing the proper entries to be made but in determining the existence of discount or premium. Basically the problem is identical with the situation in which a nonaffiliated company acquires assets against shares of its own stock. In both cases an independent evaluation of the asset acquired is needed. The practice of entering the asset at the par or stated value of the shares issued is defective in that it makes asset values dependent upon the nominal amounts assigned to capital stock. Proprietary equity is always dependent for its magnitude on the values attached to assets and debts; this holds true for an isolated transaction as well as for a company viewed as a unit. What is needed in this type of transaction, accordingly, is a fair value for the asset acquired, aside from the number of shares used and their nominal values; once the fair value is determined the question of the existence of discount or premium on the shares issued is easily answered. In a sense there has been no purchase by the parent; the former holders have merely exchanged their shares in a subsidiary for shares in the parent. In the absence of an independent appraisal of the asset acquired, barter transactions of this sort are usually dealt with by introducing a hypothetical intermediate issue of shares for cash followed by an assumed application of the cash to acquisition of the new asset. This method may yield reasonable results if an active market for the shares exists and if the number of shares used is not so large a portion of the total number outstanding as to cast doubt on the applicability to this situation of the market quotations. In the absence of these conditions and of an appraisal, the use of book value of the equity acquired seems more appropriate than par or stated value of the shares issued.

Acquisition of control of subsidiaries through a subholding company may take two forms, and a discrepancy between cost and value should be dealt with accordingly. In the first case a dominant company may acquire control through an already controlled subsidiary. If this is the situation the transaction may be viewed as though it were completed by the dominant company itself. In the absence of specific indications to the contrary it may reasonably be assumed that the subholding company acts under orders from the dominant company or at least that the parent may veto any such action proposed by a subsidiary. Under these circumstances, then, no new problem is presented; the discrepancy is dealt with in the same manner as though the dominant company had acted.

The alternative possibility is the acquisition of control of a company already a parent in its own right. The transaction is made more complex by the probability that a discrepancy already exists between the price paid by the subholding company and the book value at acquisition of its interest in its own subsidiaries. Before a solution may be formulated, the basis for setting the price paid by the top parent company must, if possible, be determined. Did the dominant company ignore as irrelevant the acquisition prices paid by the subholding company or did the parent accept the subholding company's valuation of its interest in subsidiaries? In the former case the discrepancy at issue is the difference between the cost to the dominant company and the *consolidated* book value of the controlling interest, excluding goodwill, of the group over which control is being acquired; in the latter case the discrepancy is calculated by comparing the parent's outlay with the book value of the subholding company. In the former case consolidated goodwill is a newly derived figure not including goodwill arising from the subholding company's activities; in the latter case consolidated goodwill is the goodwill evidenced by the subholding company's acquisition prices plus the additional goodwill, positive or negative, revealed by the parent's cost.[8]

As a method of determining the worth of a group of companies the former technique seems more appropriate. In examining the transaction after it has been closed, however, too much

---

8 In the special case in which the subholding company owns all the voting stock of its subsidiaries, identical solutions are obtained. Where a minority interest exists in the subsidiaries, however, differing results are forthcoming.

must not be assumed concerning methods of price determination. The facts may run counter to our own conception of sound business procedure.[9]

In large part the preceding discussion of goodwill is directly applicable to the preparation of consolidated statements at date of acquisition. If the parent enlarges or decreases its proportionate ownership of a subsidiary, need the corresponding goodwill figure be adjusted? It should be noted that the reference is to a proportionate change, not a mere change in the number of shares held. A stock dividend of common on common, for example, alters the number of shares held but not the proportion; neither does an additional issue of stock by a subsidiary which is taken *pro rata* by existing shareholders. In these and other similar cases no new discrepancy between cost and book value appears; consequently no adjustment of goodwill is required.

Under the conventional procedure of restricting goodwill to the proportion "purchased" by a parent, a new amount must be calculated each time a change in proportionate interest occurs. This requirement must follow because a change in proportionate interest occasions a change in the percentage of goodwill to be recognized. After numerous purchases and sales of a subsidiary's shares consolidated goodwill may easily become a mixture defying interpretation, except as a space filler.

When the full amount of goodwill evidenced by the price paid by a parent to acquire control is recognized no subsequent alterations are required merely as a result of changes in the number of shares held. In the event that subsequent transactions in the subsidiary's shares demonstrate a mistake in the original valuation of consolidated goodwill, or a change arising from new conditions, the whole amount should be recalculated and the revised valuation substituted for the earlier. This reappraisal is not in response to fractional shifts in a parent's proportionate holdings but to new evidence more reliable or more up-to-date than that formerly available. At any point of time, then, under this approach, consolidated goodwill represents the best estimate available of the unrecorded intangibles attaching to subsidiaries.

Apart from the problem of a change in proportionate holdings the question remains as to the propriety of carrying consolidated goodwill indefinitely. Is consolidated goodwill to be a temporary or a permanent part of the asset total? The same problem exists with respect to goodwill in a nonconsolidated balance sheet. If

---

[9] These alternative possibilities are illustrated in Accountants' handbook. Third edition: 1106–8.

goodwill is viewed as a terminable annuity, it should be amortized against revenue over its anticipated life. If the special advantages creating and sustaining goodwill are expected to persist indefinitely into the future it may be shown unimpaired in all subsequent reports.

Intercompany Bonds

The elimination of intercompany holdings of bonds and notes presents difficulties only if premium or discount is involved. Assume that Company S issued $100,000 of 10-year bonds to the public for $105,000. Five years later Company P, the parent of S, acquires for cash half the issue for $51,000. From a consolidated viewpoint, half the debt has been paid off—cash has left the group and, at maturity, payment of the block held by P will be effectuated by a shift of cash from S to P, but no cash will leave the consolidation. Since P may "sell" the bonds—i.e., borrow against them without the necessity of creating a new bond issue—they should be kept "alive" and in a consolidated balance sheet their elimination reflected by the subtraction of the bonds held intercompany from the total originally issued by S, rather than by an exhibit of merely the net amount owed outsiders.

The elimination, however, cannot be made without adjustment. Assuming straight-line amortization of premium, the bonds are carried on P's books at $102,500; one-half of the issue has a book value, then, of $51,250. Since P paid out $51,000, attempted elimination leaves a balance of $250. The cause of the discrepancy lies in the retirement of a debt carried at $51,250 for a cash outlay of $51,000; a book "gain" of $250 has resulted, exactly as in the parallel case of a nonaffiliated company acquiring its own obligations at less than book value. In the absence of further data, however, the nature and assignment of the gain are not clear. The rate of amortization of premium, for example, may have been too slow; if so, the gain is in reality a correction of past understatements by S of net income. Alternatively, a decline in bond prices may have enabled the purchaser, in this case Company P, to realize the gain. If the useful fiction may be employed that the purchaser acts as agent for the issuer the gain is always assignable to the issuer. In any event consolidated capital increases; the allocation to controlling and minority interests is dependent on the assignment of the gain to P or to S.

The proposition is sometimes advanced that a low market price for a corporation's bonds implies a revaluation of the company's assets. In the example presented above, accordingly, the excess of the book value of the indebtedness of S retired over the cash laid out by P becomes an unassigned deduction from the assets of the issuing corporation, Company S. Unquestionably there are occasions when this interpretation is superior to that of gain.

As long as the bonds are held within the affiliation, their subsequent history should not be permitted to affect consolidated capital. Interest accruals and payments will, of course, be eliminated as intercompany transactions. Any continued amortization of premium on the bonds held alive will likewise be neutralized in a manner similar to the treatment at acquisition. In brief, no further consolidated gains or losses may result from bonds and similar investments held intercompany.

Reciprocal Shareholdings

Reciprocal shareholdings (also described as "mutual," or "cross") present a problem somewhat similar to that of intercompany bonds. However, the conventional treatment of this problem ignores the logical requirements of the assumption of a group of business units treated "as if but one existed." Instead, there is a return to a position in which each affiliated unit becomes once more an independent entity—a position repudiating the whole underlying basis on which consolidated statements are built. Thus current accounting procedure denies participation in profits or dividends to treasury stock acquired directly by a corporation but grants such participation to treasury stock acquired through a controlled subsidiary. The inconsistency is defended by taking refuge in the convenient doctrine that the law accords rights of full participation to all outstanding shares, regardless of the relationship between legal owner and issuer. But no such doctrine is explicitly established in our body of law; as a matter of fact no authoritative statement of any sort seems to exist in either statutory or case law on the status of reciprocal shareholdings.

That shares of an affiliate held intercompany are in effect a form of treasury shares is widely recognized by writers in the law journals. After describing the technique of using corporate funds to obtain control of a corporation by acquisition of its own stock through a subsidiary, one writer states:

> This seems to have been permitted in New York. . . . However, *most courts would probably go behind the corporate entity and prevent the use of a subsidiary to evade the rule that corporations may not vote their own stock*. . . . This practice would likewise be disallowed in those states where the statutes stipulate that treasury stock may not be voted "directly or indirectly." [10]

[10] I. J. Levy, "Purchase by corporation of its own stock." 15 *Minnesota law review* 6, footnote. Italics are added.

Furthermore the identification of reciprocal holdings with treasury shares is not entirely unknown to accounting literature. W. A. Staub, L. A. Carman, and E. L. Kohler, among others, have given explicit recognition to the essential similarity.[11] Thus, despite the opinion of eminent accounting authority, the claim that mutually held shares are the equivalent of treasury shares for purposes of consolidated statements is not based on an "obvious" fallacy.[12]

How extensive the practice may be is difficult to ascertain because corporations are not likely to publicize the devices used to evade restrictions on treasury stock. Nevertheless enough evidence exists to warrant the belief that the problem possesses more than theoretical interest. E. J. B. Lewis gives four examples drawn from recent corporation reports.[13] A. Nussbaum recalls that the ill-starred Bank of the United States "a private enterprise, operating under a misleading name, had its own shares purchased in great numbers by subsidiary companies." He also refers to the German technique, prior to the collapse of 1931, of using foreign subsidiaries as "dummies," and gives numerous citations of both United States and foreign cases.[14]

Basically, an accounting problem is created by reciprocal holdings only in the presence of minority interests. If a dominant company holds, directly or indirectly, all the outstanding shares of a group, identical results are obtained whether the conventional simultaneous-equation method or the proposed treasury stock treatment is employed. In the presence of outside shareholders, however, the amount of a subsidiary's profits accruing to controlling and minority interests depends upon the method chosen.

It should be emphasized that the influence of minority interests in this situation is not identical with, for example, their significance with respect to the question of full or partial elimination of

---

11 "Consolidated financial statements," *The accountant* (London), LXXXI: 737 (Dec. 7, 1929);

"Intercorporate financial relationships," *American accountant*, XVII:106 (April 1932);

"Some tentative propositions, etc.," *Accounting review*, XIII:67. See also *Journal of accountancy*, LIX:73 (Jan., 1935), "Questions and answers department."

12 "Mutual stockholdings in consolidated statements" (Editorial) *Journal of accountancy* LXIX:5–6 (January, 1940).

13 Consolidated statements. (New York, 1942):186–7. He lists Associated Gas and Electric Company, Consolidated Edison Co. of New York, Republic Steel Corporation, and Standard Oil Company of California. These illustrations are presented by Lewis as cases in which reciprocally held shares were treated as treasury stock.

14 A. Nussbaum, "Acquisition by a corporation of its own shares," 35 *Columbia law review* 976, note 24; 984–5.

intercompany markups on inventories and fixed assets. Accordingly, the effect of minority interests may not be dismissed by an appeal to the function of a consolidated statement as a report primarily for the controlling interest. Neither the conventional nor the proposed treatment of mutually held shares affects in the slightest the total consolidated assets, debts, or capital. The differences between the two methods emerge in the *allocation* of consolidated capital to controlling and minority interests, not in the determination of its total amount. As a consequence, from the point of view of the controlling interest, the validity of the allocation made is at issue.

The effect on the group as a whole seems clear-cut. Some shares previously held outside the consolidation have been reacquired through the use of consolidated resources. Consolidated capital (in the broad sense) is definitely reduced exactly as the capital of a nonaffiliated corporation is diminished when its own shares are reacquired. The mutually held shares are definitely intercompany items and in consolidation are to be eliminated accordingly. On this aspect of the problem no important disagreement appears to exist.

In allocating the profits of a subsidiary to controlling and outside interests, however, despite this recognition of the nature of mutually held shares, conventional procedure treats them as fully outstanding by resort to simultaneous equations or some arithmetically equivalent method. Presumably this technique is based on the prevailing corporate practice of paying dividends on all "outstanding" shares. As the advocates of the conventional procedure correctly maintain, whether or not the law permits reciprocally held shares to vote is inconsequential; for accounting theory the important question is whether or not dividends on those shares are allowed.[15] As has been pointed out, the law is not clear and explicit on the status of mutual shareholdings. Accountants, in other words, have merely assumed an answer to a legal problem not explicitly solved in the law itself.

What then is the attitude to be taken? Both a legal and an accounting analysis emerge with the same result, namely, that holdings of a parent's shares by a controlled subsidiary have effects in substance identical with a parent's holding of its own shares. Clearly here is an opportunity to give definiteness to one aspect of the law of intercorporate relations. In this and related

---

15 See, for example, the letter by E. D. Alford, *Journal of accountancy*, LXVIII:400–1 (Dec., 1939). This letter contains some useful criticisms of my article, "Mutual stockholdings in consolidated statements," *loc. cit.*:227–35 (October, 1939).

problems the courts must look to accountants for guidance; men trained as specialists in legal techniques cannot be expected to supply satisfactory answers to problems involving economic and accounting analysis. The odd spectacle of accountants thumbing through legal tomes to find solutions to accounting problems raises the pertinent question of where the judges and legislators acquired their accounting knowledge. From accountants who learned their techniques from the law books? Unless accountants formulate in advance definite solutions of unsolved legal problems involving accounting and economic relationships they cannot legitimately object when a decision arising from a single special case is erected into a highly objectionable and demonstrably incorrect standard for accounting and business practice.

Specifically, accounting theory and practice and corporation law are finally in agreement as to the status of a company's reacquired shares. They possess no voting rights, are not entitled to dividends or to assets in case of dissolution, and instead of being included in assets must be shown as a deduction from proprietary equity. When shares are reacquired through the medium of a controlled subsidiary, however, the law is silent or contradictory and accounting practice views with seeming complacency the spectacle of a corporation in effect voting its own shares and directing the payment of dividends on them.[16]

The problem of devising a detailed technique for treating cross holdings as treasury shares must obviously await a clear-cut decision as to their exact status. On the assumption that treatment as treasury stock is desired, however, two possible methods may be outlined. A hypothetical exchange of shares between the parent and subsidiary may be postulated so that each company emerges from the exchange holding only its own shares. Alternatively, reimbursement by the parent of the subsidiary may be assumed for the latter's outlays on the parent company's stock, with the reacquired shares shifted on the consolidated work sheets to the parent company.[17] Under either method the adjust-

---

16 The excerpts reproduced in Lewis, *loc. cit.*, of the balance sheets of Republic Steel and Standard Oil of California have the companies' own shares listed under assets. Presumably the prohibition against including a company's own shares among assets may be ignored if title is vested in a nominee.

17 An example of the first method is worked out in "Mutual stockholdings in consolidated statements," *Journal of accountancy*, LXVIII:232–5 (October, 1939). The second method is illustrated in Accountants' handbook, Third edition: 1101–4. A variation of the first method was evidently employed explicitly, not merely as a consolidated adjustment, by Associated Gas and Electric Company. As cited by Lewis, *loc. cit.*, "the Statement of Consolidated Corporate and Capital Surplus for the year ended December 31, 1937 contained the following item as a deduction from Capital Surplus:

ments indicated are made at the date the reciprocal relationship was established, with absorption in consolidated surplus of any discrepancy between reacquisition price and book value. For periods subsequent to the establishment of mutuality the shares are held dormant and are therefore excluded in computing profits allocable to controlling and outside interests. In general the second procedure outlined seems preferable because it coincides more closely with the view that the act of a controlled subsidiary is in effect the act of the dominant company. No firm position need be taken, however, until all possible alternatives are explored and compared.

Assets Obtained From Affiliates

When inventories, as they appear on the books of the constituent companies, are combined the effect of intercompany markups and markdowns must be eliminated. This requirement follows the general principle of elimination of purely intercompany transactions. On the assumption that the inventories are to be reflected in a consolidated balance sheet at cost, computations must be made in terms of cost to the area of integrated operations—the entity to which the consolidated statement refers. As in the case of a single company, cost to the entity of assets and services obtained from outsiders is typically calculated as the cash outlays made or promised plus the cash value of any other consideration employed. This concept of cost includes transportation charges as legitimate components of the value of assets acquired. As a consequence packing and shipping costs on intercompany transfers of assets may be properly included in computing cost to the consolidation. "Under an ideal treatment, in fact, all charges actually incurred from the standpoint of the consolidated entity, and reasonably applicable to goods on hand in the group as opposed to goods sold to the outside, should be deferred. In other words, the amount to be eliminated as unrealized is the element of net income, not gross markup over assigned production cost." [18]

A similar redefinition of the other fundamental accounting concepts is also necessary. "Revenue" and "expense," for example, now refer to the affiliated group as a unit; therefore, when it is stated that the revenues are, in the main, to be recognized on a sales basis, the reference is to the revenue of the group and the

---

"Carrying value of subsidiary companies' investments in stocks of Associated Gas and Electric Company written off in consolidation and consolidated adjustments due to conversion of intercorporately-held convertible obligations into such stock . . . $135,772,576.15"

[18] Accountants' handbook. Third edition: 1092–3.

sales of the group. A sale does not occur, then, until a valid contract has been concluded with legal persons outside the affiliation. Mere transfers between units of the consolidated area are considered incapable of establishing gain or loss.

Full compliance with the principle of intercompany eliminations requires the cancellation of all intercompany markups and markdowns (in the sense of net profit), regardless of the relative sizes of the controlling and outside interests. Once the existence of an integrated area has been established, the proportionate equities held by controlling and outside interests are of importance in allocating consolidated capital and consolidated net income, but not in determining their amounts. The number of shares held by outsiders is ignored until the accounting for consolidated assets, debts, capital, and profits has been completed; then, and only then, do the relative interests attain significance.

The alternative procedure of limiting the elimination to the controlling interest's share of intercompany markups and markdowns is clearly at variance with the conception of consolidated statements as accounting projections of a business entity composed of numerous legal units. Concretely, the objectionable nature of partial elimination is strikingly illustrated by its effect on consolidated assets. Inventories, for example, will be shown as the sum of two types of noncomparable amounts, namely, cost to the whole entity for the portion from which intercompany adjustments have been eliminated and cost to a specific legal unit for the part retaining markups and markdowns. The result is an inventory figure defying interpretation: it is not at cost to the consolidation, nor at cost to the affiliated units, nor at market or any other conventional basis to either. It is a number without significance to anyone interested in the consolidated group or in any specified member of the group. It is, in the most invidious connotation of the phrase, a "mere bookkeeping entry."

The plea is made that this alternative procedure is valid because from the point of view of the minority interest profit on intercompany sales is definitely established. This is undoubtedly correct, but of what importance is the contention in consolidation? Consolidated statements are not prepared because of the presence of minority interests but in spite of their existence. Of course the minority is entitled to regard profits on intercompany sales as definitely established and admissible as a basis for dividends; the statements of the legal unit in which they hold shares will reflect those sales and the resultant profits. The statements of these individual units are the sources of information on these points. But consolidated statements are not prepared for the use of a minority interest and consequently the argument may not be considered as pertinent to the problem.

The conflict under discussion may be made more vivid by a simple example. Company P, controlling Company S, has on hand materials purchased from S for $100,000. The total cost to S of these materials was $80,000. In consolidation, two cost figures are present: $80,000 for S, $100,000 for P. In recording consolidated assets at cost to the affiliation, the markup of $20,000 is ignored and the materials are listed at $80,000. If, however, effect is given to the size of the minority interest, a whole series of "costs" are derived. For example, a 10 per cent minority interest in S results in an inventory figure of $82,000; a 15 per cent interest, $83,000; a 20 per cent interest, $84,000; and so on. But nothing has changed with respect to the material being valued—the outlays made by S and P have not changed, the quantities transferred and held have not changed, nothing with respect to the *materials* has changed—yet a new cost figure is obtained for every different hypothetical size of the minority interest. Surely the proportion in which shares in capital are distributed has nothing to do with the *value* to be assigned to inventories. To permit assets to assume different values merely on the basis of differing amounts of minority interest is clearly inconsistent with a rational accounting.

The point is sometimes made, particularly with reference to the influence of minority interests, that a consolidated statement may reasonably involve compromises. In one sense this contention is valid. But a compromise of an accounting proposition may take two forms, namely, (1) a modification of an ideal procedure as a concession to practical difficulties and to the peculiarities of specific situations, and (2) a refusal to take a position, with the consequent necessity of assuming at least two positions at once. A compromise of the first type is acceptable; one of the second type is not. The former implies acceptance of the "correct" or ideal solution, but sanctions a deviation as a result of human or technical imperfections. The latter fails to indicate any solution at all, except in a narrow, formalistic sense, and consequently rarely satisfies anyone. The present attempt to develop a consistent theory of consolidated statements must strive to avoid the second type of compromise, with only incidental attention to the first type. By way of contrast a handbook or manual of procedure would reverse the emphasis, at least to the extent of giving serious consideration at each point to the probable practical limitations confronting a practitioner. For example, in the earlier discussion of cancellation of intercompany shareholdings, no reference was made to the use of the phrase "excess of cost of investment in subsidiary over corresponding book value at date of acquisition" as a substitute for consolidated goodwill. The reason for the omission is that the phrase merely labels an unassigned debit, and in no way enlightens the reader of the statement as to its precise nature. Consequently the use of the phrase is no solution of the problem. As a caption to be employed, however, by an accountant who has tried to find a rational explanation for the differences between price paid and book value, and who finds no evidence of goodwill or of undervaluation of specific assets of subsidiaries, the noncommital phrase is acceptable to indicate an amount held in suspense pending a determination of its proper disposition. In this usage the compromise constitutes no denial of an ideal solution; it is not proposed as a final determination. What must be avoided, however, is the assumption that the use of a suspense account is proper in the sense of constituting a definitive solution.

The computation of consolidated cost of goods sold is consistent with the treatment of inventories outlined above. The elimination of intercompany purchases removes one important source of overstatement resulting from the summation of the unadjusted accounts of constituent companies. The elimination of intercompany markups and markdowns from beginning and ending inventories will complete the task of adjusting cost of goods sold to a consolidated basis.

The status accorded intercompany markups in inventories held at date of acquisition is not uniform. One group supports the retention in consolidation of these initial amounts; another group contends that these markups should be eliminated in exactly the same manner as markups at subsequent dates. The first group bases its position on the ground that no intercompany transactions can occur prior to affiliation, and that consequently no markups resulting from intercompany transfers exist at that time. It is also argued that the price paid for the stock of the subsidiary is based upon the market value of the assets, including inventories, and not upon costs, and hence that all elements of profit already accrued are reflected in the investment account. According to the opposing view, complete elimination of intercompany profits, in both beginning and concluding inventories, is required by the nature of consolidated statements, as otherwise they will be affected by movements of goods between units of the combination. Those in this camp question the assumption that the market value of inventories will be reflected in the price of the shares later acquired. For example, Company A sells materials to a regular customer, Company B. Later, A acquires control of B. In setting its price for the shares of B, why should A value the materials it sold to B at selling price rather than cost? "What happens is that the parent company A is accepting a return . . . of goods which it had previously thought were definitely sold and are now coming back as an incident of the acquisition of the ownership of B." [19] It may also be noted that noncancellation of intercompany profits in opening inventories impairs the comparability of an initial consolidated statement with subsequent statements. If consolidated net income of the first period is computed with initial markups retained the initial net income reported, other things being equal, will be smaller than that of the subsequent periods because the latter periods have not been dealt with on a basis consistent with the first. The entity approach, on balance, seems to favor complete elimination of markups at acquisition, as well as those in subsequent inventories.

A minor problem is that of the proper classification to be employed in consolidated balance sheets for inventories. In strict compliance with the consolidated point of view all assets which will receive further processing within the group qualify as materials or work in process, regardless of the captions employed by the constituent units; all assets destined for sale to outsiders, regardless of the status of the legal owner as parent or subsidiary, are to be listed as finished goods. As between materials and work in process, the proper line of cleavage seems to run between (a) materials newly acquired from the outside by any affiliate and (b) all other materials not classifiable as finished goods. Since classification in this manner will probably cut across the lines already established—the finished goods account of one unit, for example, may comprise commodities held in part for sale and in part for transfer to affiliated companies—the problem of reallocation may involve more effort than is justified by the results. In such cases, using the categories already present on the books is an acceptable compromise. Where the breakdown of inventories into the three customary subgroups is to be used as a basis of detailed analysis, however, reclassification is necessary to avoid drawing improper conclusions as to the relative importance of materials, work in process, and finished goods.

Save for one additional important item the disposition of intercompany markups on fixed assets is identical with the treatment developed for inventories. The entire net markup is to be elim-

---

19 W. A. Staub, "Some difficulties arising in consolidated financial statements." *Journal of accountancy*, LIII:29, (January, 1932).

inated for reasons already adduced. The additional element, the treatment of depreciation in consolidation, exists because fixed assets typically remain in the group through many accounting periods. Furthermore, depreciation will, in all probability, be recorded by the holder of the asset on the basis of its cost, not on cost to the affiliated group. The result is a characteristic overstatement, from the consolidated point of view, of both depreciation and book value of fixed assets. The remedy in principle is clear: book value should be adjusted to cost to the affiliation less depreciation on that cost, and depreciation corrected to reflect amortization of cost to the group. In the case of a group of trading companies, given the existence of records adequate to permit the computation of intercompany markups, the required adjustments are not difficult. In those cases, depreciation appears as an expense; once adjusted it is disposed of finally and completely. If the asset is used in manufacturing operations, however, the problem may become most difficult. Not only is depreciation then capitalized in work in process or finished goods but may also be embodied in transfers of finished goods to affiliates. To trace through these ramifications completely may defy the skill and ingenuity of the best-qualified staff. Under these circumstances, beyond the first transfer of the cost of the fixed asset, the use of estimates to remove intercompany markups is probably all that may reasonably be expected.[20]

It is in connection with problems of this nature that the recommendation of separate books of account for consolidated operations acquires great force. Such a set of records would account explicitly for the area of integrated operations as a single accounting unit. Costs would appear on a strictly consolidated basis, freed of any trace of intercompany markups or markdowns, and the consequent necessity imposed under conventional procedure of tracing through complex intercompany transfers would be avoided. Recommendation has been made elsewhere by others for an eliminations ledger as a device for simplifying consolidation.[21] The procedure envisaged here goes beyond the eliminations ledger to a full-blown independent set of records. How far this practice might be carried as a practical operating device is difficult to ascertain. But extensive experience covering many years is available from companies operating numerous branches.

---

20 A similar difficulty exists with respect to intercompany transfers of inventories. The eliminations required by the first transfer may usually be computed without great difficulty. However, subsequent intercompany transfers of the same materials after processing may make it impossible to trace through the resultant flow of intercompany profits.

21 For example Kohler, *Accounting review*, XIII:66 (March, 1938).

The devices employed there to give a unified accounting projection might prove well adapted to the analogous problem of consolidation. If the additional clerical costs could be held within reason the resultant increased accuracy of consolidated reports would well repay the effort. In any event the proposal is worth consideration and, perhaps, even some experimentation on a limited scale.

VI

OUTSIDE INTERESTS — CONSOLIDATED SURPLUS

Outside Interests

MINORITY INTERESTS are ever-present reminders that a completely unified area of integrated operations does not exist.[1] As a consequence the framing of a coherent consolidation procedure based on the assumption of centralized control and integrated operations gives rise to unavoidable disputes concerning the relative importance to be accorded outside interests. The position taken here is that a minority interest should not affect the determination of the magnitude of consolidated assets, debts, or total capital. This is exemplified by the treatment accorded consolidated goodwill and intercompany markups in assets. In those cases it is recommended that the values assigned be determined without consideration of the size of minority interest. This treatment is necessary to relate the consolidated statement to a specific entity, the area of integrated operations. To permit the value of consolidated inventories and cost of goods sold, for example, to be in part a function of the size of minority interests is to make the resultant magnitudes refer to two entities—the consolidated group and the subsidiary selling the commodities. This is both illogical and unnecessary; for consolidated assets and debts, a minority may be treated in the same manner as a controlling interest, which is tantamount to saying that its existence is ignored.

In the determination of the apportionment of consolidated net income and capital, however, as opposed to the calculation of their total amounts, the relative importance of the minority may not be ignored. Provision must therefore be made for the two aspects of the problem, namely, the division of consolidated net income be-

[1] Logically the term "minority" interest is unsatisfactory because it implies a quantitatively inferior position. For example, Company P owns 70 per cent of the stock of S; in turn S owns 70 per cent of T's shares. Company P's interest in T is 49 per cent; the "minority" has a 51 per cent equity—30 per cent held directly by outside shareholders of T, and 21 per cent (30 per cent of 70 per cent) held indirectly by outside shareholders of S. Nonquantitative terms such as outside, extra-group, or noncontrolling interest are logically superior. Because the term minority interest is so well entrenched, however, a terminological innovation has been avoided in this monograph by employing the more familiar phrase, with "outside" interest used frequently as the least novel synonym. A similar terminological difficulty exists with respect to preferred shares not held intercompany.

tween controlling and outside interests, and a correlative allocation of consolidated capital.

The most direct method of assuring a proper apportionment of net income is to make as many consolidated adjustments as possible against the accounts of the individual companies involved, not against the categories employed in the consolidated reports. For example, if Company P holds inventory acquired from its subsidiary, S, at a markup of $15,000, inventory of P and net income of S, rather than consolidated surplus, should be reduced by that amount. The computation of an assumed 10 per cent minority interest in S is then made on the basis of 10 per cent of the net income reported by S diminished by the $15,000 of intercompany markups eliminated.

Those who wish to retain in consolidated statements as much information as possible concerning the equity of the minority in a subsidiary's income may do so by incorporating a schedule showing minority interest at subsidiary's book value, plus or minus consolidated adjustments. In this manner the amount of "controlled" profit is made available, for whatever the information may be worth. Clearly there can be no objection to reports of this type containing more data than absolutely necessary to sustain the consolidated statements. If the minority interest is at all substantial, however, a more satisfactory arrangement is to include the statements of the subsidiary itself as an integral part of the consolidated report.

In some cases an intercompany gain or loss may not be directly assignable to a specific unit. For example, a gain on the acquisition of an affiliate's bonds at less than book value may be considered an incident of group operations rather than a gain attributable to the issuer or purchaser. In these and other similar situations a direct assignment to consolidated surplus seems the most reasonable procedure, thereby leaving minority interest unaffected. This device should not, however, be overworked. In essence this treatment assigns the whole gain or loss to the dominant company in its capacity as representative of the whole group. Until records are available for the integrated group wholly independent of the accounts of the constituent units, each adjustment made, whether it is admitted or not, is in effect a corection of the accounts of one of the affiliated companies. Consequently consolidated surplus should not be used as a dumping ground for items clearly applicable to specific companies. An example of an undesirable practice of this type is the charging of intercompany markups on inventories to consolidated surplus on the grounds that, since the minority has realized a profit, the controlling interest should assume the entire deduction. "Specifically, the inventories are shown exclusive of any element of intercompany markup, a desirable procedure; but the equities of both minority and controlling interests are distorted. Minority interest is shown at a figure applicable to the statement of a single company, not to a consolidated statement; controlling interest is shown at a figure applicable to neither type of statement." [2]

At the present time it is true that the method of allocation of consolidated net income is of little or no importance for income taxation or dividends. When consolidated returns are permitted the tax is assessed on the consolidated taxable income regardless of the size of minority interest; dividend limits are set by reference to the operations of individual companies. As a result no direct legal consequences flow from an erroneous or haphazard allocation of net income. Despite the absence of effective external pressures, an accurate apportionment should, of course, be made in order to render the statements as correct a projection as possible of consolidated affairs.

The amount of consolidated capital assigned to minority interest is then computed as the sum of the interest at the beginning of the period plus the portion of net income accruing, as described above, less dividends, plus or minus any nonconsolidated adjustments made directly to the capital accounts of the subsidiary. The minority interest is usually exhibited as the sum of the par or stated value of the shares held by outsiders plus an interest in surplus. Since the manner of reflecting the outsider's equity does not affect the total assigned, no criticism may be made of this aspect of standard procedure.[3]

The function of the magnitude assigned to minority interest in consolidated capital is to prevent an overstatement of the size of the controlling interest, not to give information to the minority. This follows from the function of a consolidated statement as an accounting projection of an integrated group, of value primarily to the management, creditors, and stockholders of the dominant company. The consolidated assets, debts, and net income shown are those of the group as a whole; consequently the consolidated capital shown is that of the entire affiliation. But in the presence

---

[2] Accountants' handbook. Third edition: 1091.

[3] For example, from the Securities and Exchange Commission's Form 10-K Instruction Book:

p. 20. "State separately, in the consolidated balance sheet, the amounts of the minority interest in the capital and in the surplus of the subsidiaries consolidated."

p. 22. "State separately in the consolidated profit and loss statement the amount of profit and loss accruing to minority interests."

of outside interests the consolidated capital may not be assigned in total to the controlling interest—to do so would result in overstatement to the extent of the equity of the minority in the consolidated picture presented.

In strict conformity with this analysis, minority interest should be shown as an explicit deduction from consolidated capital, somewhat as follows:

Total consolidated assets	$2,000,000
Total consolidated liabilities	1,000,000
Total consolidated capital	$1,000,000
Assignable to minority interest	175,000
Assignable to controlling interest	$ 825,000

The usual arrangement, however, in which controlling and minority interests are summed to show total consolidated capital is satisfactory, provided the function of minority interest is not thereby distorted. The tendency to view minority interest as a liability is clearly undesirable and the practice is logically indefensible. No obligation, as that term is used in connection with debts, exists to pay off the outside shareholders. They have no special claim against the group, the parent, or the parent's shareholders beyond the general legal right to demand that their vested interest in the *subsidiary* be respected. A claim of this nature is undoubtedly important; but it is not a debt or liability in the accounting sense.

Minority interest in consolidated capital may not be interpreted as a *proportionate* interest in the group. Even if no change occurs in the makeup of an affiliation and no change in the size of minority interest, there is no reason to expect that the relative amounts of consolidated capital assigned to outside and controlling interests will remain stable. The interest of the minority is in a portion of the group, not in the entire consolidated area; the minority's interest in consolidated capital (ignoring dividends and nonconsolidated adjustments of subsidiary capital) will vary with the profitability of closed transactions initiated by the subsidiary and concluded with persons outside the group. That equity will not be a function of the progress of the whole area of integrated operations. As a result no particular significance may be attached to the ratio of minority to controlling equity, but only to the absolute amounts involved. The prime function of minority interest must be recognized as a device for reconciling the conception of unified operations underlying consolidated statements with the presence of outside interests in some of the units.

Consolidated Surplus

Consolidated surplus is the excess of consolidated capital, defined as the difference between consolidated assets and debts, over the sum of (a) the par or stated value of the parent company's outstanding stock, and (b) minority interest.[4] At any given date, consolidated surplus is composed of the surplus of the dominant company, exclusive of any adjustments for investments in subsidiaries, plus the dominant company's equity in subsidiaries' gains or losses sustained since date of acquisition, less dividends, plus or minus consolidated adjustments not directly applicable to constituent units.[5]

The important characteristic of consolidated surplus which distinguishes it from surplus in individual balance sheets is the inclusion of subsidiaries' profits arising after acquisition by the dominant company of a controlling interest. What if a subsidiary sustains continued losses so that its liabilities exceed its assets? Limited liability of stockholders protects a parent from any legal claim to make good the deficiency in proprietary equity; consequently, the parent's investment account need not be reduced below zero. But this consideration refers to the parent's position as a legal entity, not to a consolidated projection. As long as the unprofitable company is retained as a part of the area of integrated operations, its assets and debts will enter into the corresponding totals in consolidation; inclusion in consolidated assets and liabilities requires a similar inclusion in consolidated surplus. In consolidated statements, therefore, losses will continue to be reflected through consolidated surplus, regardless of the existence of a lower limit to the parent's investment account.

In the preceding paragraphs the customary distinction between earned and capital surplus was glossed over. The extension to consolidated reports of this standard treatment of surplus requires examination of the functions performed by each type.

---

4 By contrast with the terms "consolidated assets," "consolidated liabilities," and "consolidated capital," which refer to the whole integrated area, consolidated surplus usually refers merely to the interest of the controlling group.

5 "Earned surplus in the consolidated balance sheet arising from subsidiary companies should be confined to undistributed profits earned since the date of acquisition, without regard to the period prior to that date during which an interest less than controlling may have been owned. Earned surplus applicable to shares acquired after the controlling-interest date should be computed only from the date of acquiring such shares." Kohler, *Accounting review*, XIII:67 (March, 1938).

The strategic factor is earned surplus; once that term is defined, capital surplus may be described as all surplus other than earned. Two conceptions of earned surplus are prevalent:

1. Earned surplus is a measure of dividend limits; that is, it indicates the extent to which assets are legally distributable to stockholders.
2. Earned surplus is a measure of undistributed "realized" profits; that is, it indicates the extent to which assets may be distributed without impairing capital.

The two are by no means synonymous. Wasting-asset corporations, for example, may legally impair capital in dividend distributions; under such circumstances earned surplus is no indicator of dividend limits. Furthermore, state dividend laws differ with respect to the status of paid-in surplus and the necessity of covering deficits. As a result in large part of disparate dividend laws, accounting practice tends to favor the second conception of earned surplus. Whether this tendency clarifies or obscures accounting reports cannot be determined here. It is sufficient for the present purpose to note the two alternatives and apply the apparent choice of accountants to consolidated reports.

Both because of the accounting emphasis on earned surplus as undistributed realized profit and because of legal opposition to basing dividends on consolidated results, the second interpretation is more appropriate to consolidated statements.[6] The obvious corollary is that consolidated earned surplus may not be interpreted as a measure of short-term dividend policy. It may be viewed as an indicator of the progress of the affiliation as a whole from the date when centralized control and unified operations began. Quantitatively, consolidated earned surplus is the difference between (a) the controlling interest's share in profits realized by the consolidation since date of acquisition, plus the dominant company's earned surplus at that time, and (b) dividends appropriated to the dominant company's shareholders after that date.

In order to provide a maximum of information to a dominant company's shareholders, consolidated surplus may be shown according to a threefold classification: (a) earned surplus from the dominant company's records, unadjusted for changes in subsidiaries (this category reflects undistributed net income of the dominant company viewed as a separate legal entity) (b) equity in subsidiaries' gains or losses (the sum of (a) and (b) consti-

[6] See, for example, Cintas v. American Car and Foundry Co., 131 N.J.Eq. 419, 25 A.2d 418 (1942).

tutes consolidated earned surplus); and (c) consolidated capital surplus, comprising valid components of consolidated capital not reflected elsewhere and arising from transactions not ordinarily considered as establishing realized gains or losses.

Additional information may be incorporated by the use of subclasses under each major group indicated, by running comments in the body of the consolidated statement, by footnotes, or by reference to the statements of individual companies. The disposal of a parent's or subsidiary's earned surplus may be legally restricted, for example, by the sinking fund provisions of a bond indenture or by the treasury stock sections of the corporation law; it may be voluntarily restricted by reserves for contingencies, for preferred stock redemption, or for anticipated price declines. Strictly speaking, such earmarking of surplus is properly reflected in individual statements, but may be shown in consolidated reports as well. As long as the nature of each item is clearly indicated, and as long as the subgroups are mere divisions of major categories, no logical objections may be offered to the inclusion of additional detail. The major theoretical problem is to provide the framework, to indicate the minimum structure required to complete the skeleton. The problem of detailed presentation, the process of converting the framework into a full-blown representation of a specific economic entity, is a task requiring intelligent treatment of the data pertinent to each individual case.

VII

SUMMARY AND CONCLUSIONS

BY THE ADOPTION of a single leading premise as to the function of consolidated statements, a consistent theory to support and guide the compilation of multicompany reports has been derived. The assumption that consolidated statements are best fitted to reflect, on the accounting level, the affairs of an entity composed of a group of closely affiliated companies was based upon an appeal to the historical circumstances shaping their adoption and growth. The distinctive pattern assumed by the combination movement in this country made necessary the invention of an accounting technique to match the new business forms. In the molding of this technique, conflicting requirements of the law, of prevailing corporate practices, of conventional accounting procedures, and of pressures generated in specific cases combined to bring about a confusing array of prescriptive rules for the preparation and presentation of consolidated reports. It has been the contention of this monograph that a coherent theory, capable not merely of rationalizing some of the practices already prevalent but competent to solve new problems as they arise, must be based on rigorous, single-minded attention to the one function which can be performed by consolidated statements better than by any other known accounting device.

The clarity gained by confining consolidated statements to one well-defined purpose is matched by sharp limitation as to use. They may not legitimately be offered as all-purpose reports capable of informing every group with an interest in some special phase of consolidated operations; they may be offered to and used by those groups with an interest in the whole area of combined activity. Typically, these groups will be confined to the dominant stockholders, present and prospective, and to the managerial group wielding centralized control. Others may conceivably derive some value from these specialized reports but they must not expect too much.

The direct consequence of limited purpose is relegation to an essentially supporting role in the hierarchy of financial reports. The legal statements of the important constituent units are not supplanted but rather supplemented by consolidated statements. This will be true as long as the individual affiliated corporations are legally superior to the whole area of integrated operations for purposes such as dividends and liability for debts. If the future brings an alteration in this relationship, consolidated statements will be correspondingly elevated or depressed in importance.

Reliance on consolidated reports by interested groups imposes a dual obligation on accountants both to insist on their preparation whenever an area of integrated operations exists and to withhold them in the absence of that essential condition. The determination of the exact boundaries of an integrated area may be difficult, but it should rarely prove impossible. Consolidated statements have been developed primarily as accounting projections of consolidations through stock ownership; consequently, a potential combination of this type is indicated by intercompany shareholdings. When these shareholdings are found in conjunction with centralized control and closely integrated operations the conditions essential to consolidated statements are present.

The leading principle in the technique of preparing consolidated statements is the elimination of all evidences of intercompany relationships. This principle is universally acknowledged and, for the most part, adhered to in practice. The objective attained by elimination is the suppression of amounts and accounts reflecting transactions among the constituent units and the retention of only those data pertinent to the showing of the affiliation as an economic or business entity. In essence this requires a shift in viewpoint from that of a legal abstraction—the business corporation—to that of an accounting abstraction—the effective business unit. The shift must be made, and it must be complete.

As to the major controversial issues in consolidation, arising for the most part from disagreement as to the specific application of the principle of elimination, the conclusions derived may be summarized as follows:

1. Accounts reflecting ownership of an affiliate's shares may well record the fluctuations in the owners' equity revealed by the audited statements of the company in which the investment is held. The effects of dividends, reorganizations, and other alterations of subsidiary equity may then be reflected by appropriate changes in the investment accounts.

2. In the published reports of subsidiaries it is desirable to distinguish—as far as practicable—between transactions with affiliates and those with outsiders. Minority interests and creditors are then equipped to judge the results of affiliation on the subsidiary.

3. Assets obtained from affiliates must be shown at cost (or other conventional basis) to the entire affiliation viewed as an accounting unit, regardless of the size of minority interest. Specifically, this calls for inclusion of inventories and fixed assets at amounts freed of any trace of intercompany net gains or losses. Likewise, cost of goods sold and depreciation should be included on a fully consolidated basis not influenced by minority interest.

4. Insofar as acquisition prices sustain a finding of previously unrecorded intangible values, such values should be shown in full. Intangibles already recorded, not arising out of acquisition of subsidiaries, are to be retained.

5. Bonds and similar liabilities held by affiliates are to be eliminated as treasury bonds at the date the intercompany holdings occurred, and discount or premium disposed of accordingly.

6. Mutual shareholdings should logically be treated as treasury items. The law, for all practical purposes, is silent on this matter, and prevailing corporate practices are evidently in conflict. Accountants should advocate strongly a treatment in law and corporation procedure consistent with the nature of the transaction involved.

7. Consolidated statements are prepared despite the presence of minority interests. Minority equity must be indicated, however, to avoid an overstatement of the size of the controlling equity. Minority interests in consolidated capital and income are to be computed after consolidated adjustments are made, and not on the basis of a subsidiary's unadjusted records.

Though all actual or potential difficulties arising in connection with consolidated statements have obviously not been covered in this monograph, the underlying theory has been elaborated and its application to the leading controversies discussed in sufficient detail to illustrate the manner of its application to other phases of the problem. The lack of attention to the technical and mechanical difficulties associated with the construction of multicompany reports is in no wise intended to suggest that these matters are unimportant; it is believed, however, that the task of compilation is made easier when based on a clear view of the intended objective. The useful application of this or any other theory is still dependent upon the ingenuity and good judgment of those who deal with the baffling cross-currents of concrete situations.

*

BIBLIOGRAPHY

American institute of accountants. "Foreign operations and foreign exchange." *Accounting research bulletin no. 4.* (New York, 1939).

Anderson, W. H., Limitations of the corporate entity. (St. Louis, 1931).

Aveyard, C. H. "Consolidated balance sheets," *The accountant*, XCVIII:876–8 (June 25, 1938).

Bell, W. H., Accountants' reports. (New York, 1934).

Berle, A. A., Cases and materials in the law of corporation finance. (St. Paul, 1930).

———, Studies in the law of corporation finance. (Chicago, 1928).

Berle, A. A., and Means, G. C., The modern corporation and private property. (New York, 1932).

Binder, B. H., "Holding companies' profit and loss accounts," *The accountant*, LXXXVIII:633–9 (May 13, 1933).

Boedeker, M. J., "Elimination of intercompany profits from consolidated statements," *American accountant*, XV:111–4 (March, 1930).

Bonbright, J. C., and Means, G. C., Holding companies. (New York, 1932).

———, "Holding companies—United States," *Encyclopedia of the social sciences*, VII:403–9. (New York, 1932).

Bores, W., "Geschichtliche Entwicklung der konsolidierten Bilanz," *Zeitschrift für handelswissenschaftliche Forschung*, XXVIII:113–6; 209–22; 327–36 (March, April, June, 1934).

Brundage, P. F., "Some shortcomings in consolidated statements," *Journal of accountancy*, L:285–92 (October, 1930).

Burtchett, F. F., Corporation finance. (New York, 1934).

Byrd, K. F., "The preparation of consolidated balance sheets of holding and subsidiary companies," *The accountant*, CI:654–60; 677–81 (December 16 and 23, 1939).

California, State of. The Corporations Code. Adopted 1947.

Carman, L. A., "Intercorporate relationships," *American accountant*, XVII:-103–8; 140–2; 171–7; 204–12 (April, May, June, July, 1932).

Carson, G. C., "Elimination of intercompany profits in consolidated statements," *Journal of accountancy*, XXXVI:1–6; 390–1 (July, November, 1923).

Cash, W., "Consolidated balance sheet," *The accountant*, LXXXI:725–30 (December 7, 1929). Paper presented at International Congress on Accounting, New York, Sept., 1929.

Chantrey, W. H., "Some points arising under the Companies Act, 1929," *The accountant*, LXXXVIII:533–8 (April 22, 1933).

Childs, W. H., Consolidated financial statements: principles and procedures. (Ithaca, 1949).

"Classification of loss by subsidiary," *Journal of accountancy*, LXII:226–7 (September, 1936).

"Consolidated accounts," *The accountant*, LXXXI:713–5 (December 7, 1929).

"Consolidated balance sheets," *The accountant*, LXXII:926 (June 6, 1925). The correspondence between Brunner and Garnsey.

"Consolidated balance-sheets" (editorial), *Journal of accountancy*, XL:37–40 (July, 1925).

"Consolidating inventories," *Haskins and Sells bulletin*, (July, 1924).

"Consolidation of balance-sheets of domestic corporations with those of foreign subsidiary," *Journal of accountancy*, LXIII:298 (April, 1937).

Cooper, S. R., "Auditing of concerns," *The accountant*, XCIX:461–7 (October 1, 1938).

Cross, M. C., Types of business enterprise. (New York, 1928).

Cutforth, A. E., Amalgamation schemes. (London, 1920).

———, Methods of amalgamation. (London, 1926).

Daniels, M. B., Financial statements. American accounting association monograph no. 2. (Chicago, 1939).

de Paula, F. R. M., "The form of presentation of the accounts of holding companies," *The accountant*, XCI:853–60 (December 15, 1934).

Dewing, A. S., The financial policy of corporations. 2 vols. (New York, 1941).

"The Dunlop accounts," *The accountant*, XC:651–2 (May 12, 1934).

"Dunlop's new standard," *ibid.*:676–9.

Eggleston, D. C., Modern accounting theory and practice. (New York, 1930).

Ferguson, W. S., and Crocombe, F. R., Limited companies and their accounts. (Toronto, 1932).

Finney, H. A., Principles of accounting. vol. 2 (Advanced). (New York, 1934).

———, "Mutual stock holdings," *Journal of accountancy*, XXXIII:368–84 (May, 1922).

———, "Minority interest," *ibid.*:138–9 (February, 1922).

———, "Goodwill in consolidated balance-sheet," *ibid.*:63–4 (January, 1922).

———, "Sale of subsidiary stock by holding company," *ibid.* XXXV:461 (June, 1923).

Finney, H. A., and Baumann, H. P., "Consolidated goodwill in relation to minority interest," *ibid.* XLIV:460–3 (December, 1927).

"Foreign operations and foreign exchange," *ibid.* LXXI:27 (January, 1941).

Garnsey, G. F., Holding companies and their published accounts. Third edition. (London, 1936).

Gerstenberg, C. W., and Johnson, W. S., Organization and control. (New York, 1917).

Great Britain. Finance (No. 2) Act, 1915. Companies Act, 1929.

Greidinger, B. B., Accounting requirements of the Securities and Exchange Commission. (New York, 1940).

Hanson, A. W., Problems in auditing. (New York, 1930).

Hatfield, H. R., Accounting—Its Principles and Problems. (New York, 1927).

Hilton, J., A study of trade organisations and combinations in the United Kingdom. (London, 1920).

Hoffmann, A., Die Konzernbilanz. (Leipzig, 1930).

Husband, G. R., "The corporate-entity fiction and accounting theory," *Accounting review*, XIII:241–52 (September, 1938).

Hynning, C. J., Taxation of corporate enterprise. U. S. Temporary National Economic Committee. Monograph no. 9. (Washington, D.C., 1941).

"Inter-company profits," *The accountant*, LXXXVIII:566 (April 20, 1933).

Jones, J. W., "The consolidated return," *Journal of accountancy*, LV:255–71 (April, 1933).

Kerr, D. S., "Consolidated balance sheets," *The accountant*, LIII:627–30 (November 20, 1915).

Kester, R. B., Advanced accounting. (New York, 1933).

Kohler, E. L., "Some tentative propositions underlying consolidated reports," *Accounting review*, XIII:63–76 (March, 1938). Comments by H. T. Scovill, *ibid.*:73–6.

Kracke, E. A., "Consolidated financial statements," *Journal of accountancy*, LXVI:372–89 (December, 1938).

Latty, E. R., Subsidiaries and affiliated corporations. (Chicago, 1936).

Le Clear, W. M., "Consolidated balance-sheets and contingent liabilities," *Journal of accountancy*, XLII:12–16 (July, 1926).

Levy, I. J., "Purchase by corporation of its own stock," *Minnesota law review*, XV:1–39 (December, 1930).

Lewis, E. J. B., Consolidated statements. (New York, 1942).

Liefmann, R., "Holding companies—Europe," in *Encyclopedia of the social sciences*, VII:409–11. (New York, 1932).

"Minority interests on consolidated balance-sheets," *Journal of accountancy*, LXII:227–8 (September, 1936).

Montgomery, R. H., Auditing theory and practice. 6th edition. (New York, 1940).

Moonitz, M., "The entity approach to consolidated statements," *Accounting review*, XVII:236–42 (July, 1942).

———, "Mutual stockholdings in consolidated statements," *Journal of accountancy*, LXVIII:227–35 (October, 1939); correspondence, *ibid.*:400–1 (December, 1939); editorial, *ibid.* LXIX:5–6 (January, 1940).

Morgan, H., "Holding companies' accounts," *The accountant*, XCIV:285–6 (February 22, 1936).

Newlove, G. H., Consolidated balance sheets. (New York, 1926).

———, Consolidated statements, including mergers and consolidations (New York, 1948).

———, "Step-by-step procedure in preparing consolidated balance sheets," *American accountant*, XIV:73–6 (February, 1929).

Nussbaum, A., "Acquisition by a corporation of its own shares," *Columbia law review*, XXXV:971–1006.

Palmour, C. J. G., "Auditing of concerns," *The accountant*, XCIX:493–9 (October 8, 1938).

Paton, W. A., Advanced accounting. (New York, 1941).

———, (Editor). Accountants' handbook. Third edition. (New York, 1943).

Powell, F. J., Parent and subsidiary corporations. (Chicago, 1931).

Robson, T. B., "The construction of consolidated accounts—some points to be taken into consideration," *The accountant*, XCIV:364–81 (March 7, 1936). Editorial comment, *ibid.*:345–7.

———,"Some holding company problems," *ibid.*, XCV:57–60 (July 11, 1936).

Saliers, E. A., "Considerations of consolidated accounts, *Administration*, I:773–82 (June, 1921).

Sanders, T. H., Hatfield, H. R., and Moore, U., Statement of accounting principles. (New York, 1938).

Scott, D. R., "A simplified solution of circuit ratio problems," *Accounting review*, XVIII:99–103 (April, 1943).

Seager, H. R., and Gulick, C. A., Jr., Trust and corporation problems. (New York, 1929).

Seatree, W. E., "Consolidated balance sheets" (correspondence), *The accountant*, LXXXII:20–1 (January 4, 1930).

Seidman, J. S., "Some pitfalls of consolidated balance-sheets," *Robert Morris associates monthly bulletin*, August, 1935:56–9.

Shobe, P. L., "Surplus at date of acquisition," *Haskins and Sells bulletin*, XI:58–61 (August, 1928).

Simons, A. J., Holding companies. (London, 1927).

Staub, W. A., "Consolidated financial statements," *The accountant*, LXXXI:-730–41 (December 7, 1929). Paper presented to International Congress on Accounting, New York, September, 1929.

———, "Some difficulties arising in consolidated financial statements," *Journal of accountancy*, LIII:10–30 (January, 1932).

Stempf, V. H., "Consolidated financial statements," *ibid.*, LXII:358–76 (November, 1936).

"Stock of subsidiary on balance-sheet of parent company," *ibid.*, LIX:73–4 (January, 1935).

Streightoff, F. H., Advanced accounting. (New York, 1932).

Sunley, W. T., "Minority interests in intercompany profits," *Journal of accountancy*, XXXV:350–5 (May, 1923).

Sweet, H. N., "Amended requirements for financial statements prescribed by the Securities and Exchange Commission in Regulation S-X," *ibid.*, LXIX:167–74 (March, 1940).

Trouant, D. L., Financial audits. (New York, 1937).

United States. Securities Act of 1933, sec. 19(a).
Securities Exchange Act of 1934, sec. 13(b).
Securities and Exchange Commission:
Accounting series release no. 24 (May 23, 1941).
no. 32 (March 10, 1942).
no. 39 (December 19, 1942).
Instruction book for Form 10. (Government printing office.)
Instruction book for Form 10-K. (Government printing office.)
In the matter of Associated Gas and Electric Company, Securities Exchange Act of 1934, Release no. 3285A, mimeo., (Philadelphia, 1942).
In the matter of Cities Service Company, 8 S. E. C., 326.
Regulation S-X, Article 4. (Government Printing Office).
Statistics of American listed corporations, Part I. (Philadelphia, 1940).
Survey of American listed corporations. (Various studies, differently dated).

United States. Office of Price Administration. Instruction book (revised December 1, 1942) for filing Form A—Annual financial report and Form B—Interim financial report. (Government printing office, 1943).

United States. Treasury department, Bureau of internal revenue, Regulations 104, "Consolidated returns," (Government printing office, 1940); Regulations 110, "Consolidated excess profits tax regulations" (Government printing office, 1941).

Walton, S., "Interdependent variables," *Journal of accountancy*, XXIX:467–70 (June, 1920).

Walton, S., and Langer, C. H., Advanced accounting. (Chicago, 1918).

Werntz, W. W., "Some problems as to parent companies," *Journal of accountancy*, LXVII:337–41 (June, 1939).

Legal Cases:

In re Asiatic Banking Corp., L.R. 4 Ch.App. 252 (1869).
Pearson v. Railroad, 62 N.H. 537; 13 Am.St.Rep. 590 (1885).
Robotham v. Prudential Insurance Co., 46 N.J.Eq. 673; 53 Atl. 842 (1903).
Hart Steel Co. v. Railroad Supply Co., 244 U.S. 294 (1917).
Southern Pacific Co. v. Lowe, 247 U.S. 330 (1918).
Chicago, Milwaukee, and St. Paul Railway Company v. Minneapolis Civic and Commerce Association, 247 U.S. 490 (1918).
Gulf Oil Corp. v. Llewellyn, 248 U.S. 71 (1918).
U. S. v. Reading Co., 253 U.S. 26 (1920).

Legal Cases—Continued:

Majestic Co. v. Orpheum Circuit, Inc., 21 F.2d 720 (1927).

Industrial Research Corp. v. General Motors Corp., 29 F.2d 623 (1928).

Ross v. Pennsylvania Railroad Co., 106 N.J.L. 536; 148 Atl. 741 (1930).

Consolidated Rock Products Co. v. du Bois, 312 U.S. 510 (1941).

Cintas v. American Car and Foundry Co., 131 N.J.Eq. 419; 25 A.2d 418 (1942).

INDEX

Page

Accounting propositions, compromise of ... 71–72
Armco International Corporation ... 21

Bad debts, intercompany ... 41
Bethlehem Steel Co. ... 24, 29
bond issue, guarantee of ... 43
bonds, intercompany, see "debts, intercompany long-term".
branch accounting ... 40, 74

Cambria Iron Co. ... 24
capital, consolidated ... 42, 65, 79
  apportionment of ... 76–77
capital stock, discount or premium on ... 61
Chicago, Milwaukee and St. Paul Ry. v. Minneapolis Civic & Commerce Ass'n ... 5
Cintas v. American Car and Foundry ... 6, 15
Clayton Act of 1914 ... 2
consistency ... 19, 36
consolidated operations, books of account for ... 74
consolidated returns ... 7–8, 9
consolidated statements
  as statistical exhibit ... 16
  auxiliary nature of ... 12
  partnership concept of ... 17
  statistical supplements to ... 17
  status in
    England ... 9
    Europe ... 9
    United States ... 6–11
Consolidated Rock Products v. du Bois ... 5, 12
consolidating statement ... 45
control
  centralized ... 21, 24, 29
  minority ownership and ... 23–26
  temporary ... 22, 23, 37
controlled companies, investment in nonintegrated ... 30, 34, 35
controlling interest, importance of consolidated reports to ... 15, 17
corporation laws, diverse ... 32
cost of goods sold, consolidated ... 72
creditors, long-term ... 13
  short-term ... 13
cross-holdings, see "treasury stock".

Debts, intercompany long-term ... 41, 64, 77
  intercompany short-term, see "receivables, intercompany" and "payables, intercompany".
depreciation ... 73–74

Page

Des Moines Union Railway Co. 24
dividends 78–80
 cumulative 55
 intercompany 6, 41, 51–2, 53
 stock 53–55
Du Pont de Nemours (E.I.) 31

Electric Time Co. 26
entity, business or economic 12, 20

Farmers' and Merchants' Bank 29
fiscal years, dissimilar 38
fixed assets, consolidated 35, 73–74
foreign exchange
 accounting for 34
 effect of restrictions on 33, 34
 instability of 35

General Electric Co. 26
General Motors Corp. 31
general overvaluation, allowance for 60
going concern, concept of 18
goodwill, consolidated 19, 57–61, 62, 63
group statement 32, 35

Hart Steel Co. v. Railroad Supply Co. 5
holding company
 advantages of 2
 antimonopoly legislation and 2
 Europe 1n
 United States 1–3

Income, parent company's 52
income tax 78
Industrial Research v. General Motors 5
Inspiration Consolidated Copper Co. 25n
interest, intercompany 41, 65
inventories, consolidated 34, 69–73, 77
investment, intercompany
 gain or loss on purchase of 56, 60
 valuation of 46–52

Ledger, eliminations 74
liabilities, contingent 42

Majestic Co. v. Orpheum Circuit 4
management fees, intercompany 42
markdowns and markups, intercompany 42, 44, 69–73
minority interest
 function of 78
 importance of consolidated reports to 13
 intercompany profits and 69–71
 liability aspect of 79

Page

minority interest—Continued
 proportionate interest aspect of 79
 quantitative importance of in U. S. 10–11
 reciprocal shareholdings and 66
 stock dividends and 54
mutual shareholdings, see "treasury stock".

Net income, consolidated, apportionment of 76–77
New Jersey, corporation law of 1
New York Stock Exchange, requirements of 9
note, editorial (by W. A. Paton) 46–47
notes, discounted 43

Office of Price Administration, requirements of 9
Outer Harbor Dock and Wharf Co. 26
outside interest, see "minority interest".

Payables, intercompany 40
process, period of 42
profit, intercompany, see "markdowns and markups, intercompany".
profits, controlled 43, 77
Public Utility Holding Company Act 14n, 19, 28
Pullman Incorporated 23, 29
Pullman-Standard Car Manufacturing Co. 29
Pullman Trust and Savings Bank 29
purchases, intercompany 41, 72

Receivables, intercompany 40
reciprocal shareholdings, see "treasury stock".
rents, intercompany 42
Robotham v. Prudential Insurance Co. 5
royalties, intercompany 42

St. Louis Car Co. 21
sales, intercompany 41–2, 43, 70
Securities and Exchange Commission, requirements of 8, 28
services, intercompany 42
shareholdings, intercompany 41, 65
shares, nonvoting 22
Sherman Act of 1890 1
shipments, freight on intercompany 69
significance, lack of 38
simultaneous equations 66, 67
standards, need for objective 20
statements, analysis of 42
stockholders, majority, see "controlling interest".
 minority, see "minority interest".
stockholdings, intercompany, see "shareholdings, intercompany".
Stone and Webster 31
subholding company 62
subsidiary corporations, legal theory of 4
subsidiaries, investment in 41, 72
 losses of 80
 reorganization of 51

Page

surplus, consolidated ____ 69, 77
  capital ____ 80–81
  earned ____ 80–81
  preacquisition ____ 52

Treasury stock
  reciprocal shareholdings as ____ 65
  status of ____ 68
turnover, rates of ____ 42

Uniform Partnership Act ____ 4
Union Oil Company ____ 26
United Chemicals, Inc. ____ 25
U. S. v. Reading Co. ____ 5
United States Rubber Co. ____ 31
United States Steel Corporation ____ 7

Valuation, primacy of asset ____ 17, 76

Warren Telechron Co. ____ 26
Westvaco Chlorine Products Corp. ____ 25
Woolworth (F. W.) Co. ____ 32

END OF VOLUME